Fish Out of Water

Navigating Dyslexia, My Faith, and Road to Fish Biology

Jeffrey S. McLain

"**F**or I know the plans I have for you," declares the LORD, "plans to prosper you and not to harm you, plans to give you hope and a future."

(Jeremiah 29:11, The Holy Bible, NIV)

Foreword

Writing this book has been a therapeutic exercise for me. It was a connect-the-dots exercise about my childhood and adulthood. Looking back at my life and learning from it is a healing process filled with lessons and discoveries.

As a child, I struggled in the classroom to such an extent that I was placed in a special day class for several years. I was moved from the neighborhood elementary school across the street from my house to a different school because I had been diagnosed with an auditory/visual-symbol processing deficit learning disability. This condition is further identified as dyslexia and, in addition, was stated as a permanent learning disability. It was difficult for me to pinpoint the exact difference in myself because dyslexia is a hidden disability. I know what you are thinking–"I have dyslexia. I switch my letters all the time." Dyslexia is a processing issue, and individuals with this condition often encounter challenges with words; however, switching letters does not necessarily indicate the presence of dyslexia. The main problem with dyslexia is the turning of print into sound. This issue can be seen in dyslexic individuals when they listen to their reading and hear the faulty results, often mispronunciations, truncated words, etc. Modern research suggests people with dyslexia show different brain structures and functions.

Common symptoms of dyslexia in children may include poor handwriting, spelling, performance on multiple-choice tests, and difficulty remembering specific facts and dates. As a child and young adult, I experienced all of these symptoms of dyslexia. While I had all the ingredients of a happy childhood, school was always challenging. I also faced a significant list of reading and communication problems. At the time, I was unsure of my future and fearful I would fail.

Because of my difficulty in school, I developed scars that lasted a very long time. I was part of a special day class funded by the California Department of Education for students with learning disabilities within the district. I was diagnosed before the passage of the Education for All Handicapped Children Act of 1975 (PL 94-142) and before the development of neuroimaging technologies that have significantly advanced our understanding and treatment of learning disabilities. It took over two decades before dyslexia was included in the list of conditions that cannot be used to discriminate against an employee, per the changes made to the Americans with Disabilities Act.

Furthermore, it took decades for me to understand that I was extremely fortunate to have been tested and diagnosed with dyslexia at an early age. The early testing of learning disorders enables early detection and care. In today's current educational environment, there is no guarantee that every child will be tested or screened for dyslexia. In fact, as of early 2023, California still does not require all young students to be screened for dyslexia.

In the first part of this book, I describe my childhood, school difficulties, and the things I did to navigate the challenging school environment. I found solace in hobbies and sports, making school bearable, and I got into college through a program for the academically disadvantaged and the college Disability Department. I graduated with a bachelor of arts degree in aquatic biology and obtained my master of arts in aquatic biology from graduate school.

In the second half of my book, I discuss my career as a federal government fish biologist and provide real-world examples of my work in the natural resources of a federal agency. I found an opportunity to work as a fish biologist with the U.S. Fish and Wildlife Service. I recognized that I could make significant contributions as an employee. During my career, I noticed some positive signs of dyslexia, including an enhanced ability to understand the big picture, a strong understanding of non-reading subjects, unusual resilience, heightened empathy for others, and improvement in technical areas. I continued to work hard and received promotions and new opportunities. I do my best to identify the potential benefits of dyslexia as I share my career.

Several other topics are a part of this book, and they may appear unrelated, but they are essential in shaping who I am today. God touched me while traveling in Europe, and I started reading the Bible. I discovered my true purpose in life is to serve God through my job and local church. I gave my life to Jesus Christ, the son of God. This book goes into my struggle with faith and science—from an academic standpoint and in the workplace. When it comes down to it, many of the stumbling blocks regarding this issue were in my head. Evolution and faith rarely came up at work. It is not as if I was an evolutionary biologist and people suddenly found out I was a Christian. Whether one believes in God, creation, or full-blown evolution is often unknown to one's colleagues unless these beliefs are expressed. Some excellent biologists are atheists, and some outstanding biologists are Christians. It was and is the most essential part of my life and should be shared. Faith in Christ is what defines me and helps me navigate life.

While this book features some entertaining stories, I intentionally omitted specific anecdotes to stay focused on the theme. Girlfriends, cars, and escapades of sorts are omitted. I chose to be brief and to share the highlights of many things. All of the stories I share are true. This doesn't remove any significant people who were part of my life growing up and helped me become who I am. In addition, I have made many lifelong friends at work, and I care deeply about them. I decided to respect their privacy and not include their names in this book.

Because some events are relatively recent, and many of my former colleagues are still working, I cannot go into much detail about some work situations. I decided to summarize the basic facts. Names have been mentioned sparingly, and in some cases, they have been changed.

Like any large organization, there are good and bad parts, and the federal government is no different. However, this book is not a review of the federal government; the federal government is and will always be an excellent place to work. This book is about my disability and how I survived and thrived. All parts of this book are my thoughts and perspectives, and the contents have not been approved or verified by the agencies I work with or for which I have worked.

For the dyslexic individuals among us, I used a dyslexic-friendly font and enlarged text to help with readability. I hope you find this book inspirational and helpful.

I wanted to provide an example of how a disability can be overcome and even strengthen someone. I hope that this book can be inspirational for those suffering from disabilities. You may look different, be a poor test taker, or not fit the average classroom crowd, but read on and see how I survived and eventually thrived. Know that many labeled as "disabled" compensate for the disability and develop unique skills and abilities as they overcome the struggles. There is a place in society for these unique skills. Have hope!

Please reach out and let me know what you think of my book. The best way to reach me is via the contact form of my author website, Jeffreymclain.com.

Contents

Chapter One

Something Was Wrong

My mom and dad moved to a small suburban neigh-borhood in Lafayette, California, in 1972. I was five years old, and my sister was three. My dad worked in San Francisco and left every day in a carpool. At the end of the day, he would share PG jokes, otherwise known as Dad Jokes, that he exchanged with his carpool buddies. For example, "I don't trust those trees. They seem kind of shady," or, "Why don't eggs tell jokes? They'd crack each other up." This was a way for him to share about his day, and we appreciated it. My sister would become a significant part of my life. We fought like brothers and sisters do, and we got closer in high school. We spent time together with friends, at the pool, watching televi-sion, and helping each other when needed.

My mom was an elementary school teacher but took time off when my sister and I were born. She didn't resume her teaching career until after I entered high school. Large plum and walnut trees in the backyard consumed my mom's summers. She was always looking for something to do with the bounty that came from those trees. She would make jam or jelly with the plums and crack walnuts endlessly. I had a fantastic childhood...when I wasn't at school.

Cell phones and computer games were yet to be developed, and most of my time was spent outdoors, exploring. We lived directly across the street from an elementary school, which provided unlimited recreational opportunities. It had a huge playground, including extensive fields, basketball hoops, tennis courts, and more. There were many things to do after school and on the weekends. The swim club down the street provided all-day-long activities during the summer. My sister and I would head to the pool in the morning for swim practice, go home and eat, and then head back to the pool and swim and play tennis the rest of the day. It was nonstop. Summer meant grape soda, sunburns, tennis, and wrinkled fingers from the pool.

There were many young kids in my neighborhood. Large groups of us would have free play in the afternoons. Even during summer afternoons when we weren't at the pool, I remember playing games like wiffle ball, kickball, tug-of-war, and hide-and-seek. I remember playing in the weeds across the street. The enormous mustard weeds were so tall they appeared like trees as we crawled on our bellies through them to hide from each other. Many of the older kids became people I looked up to.

I started kindergarten across the street at the elementary school. I remember the exact classroom and the little playground attached. My teacher had us do many crafts, including cutting and pasting items. I remember I didn't like one of my crafts, and I threw it away, and she made me pull it out of the trash. This little memory has stuck with me.

My parents had a yellow Oldsmobile when I was a kid. They also had an old Volkswagen bus with a sink. I don't remember lots of conversations in the house, but I do remember talking and listening a lot in the car—especially when we were driving to southern California to see our cousins. Life seemed very normal until a conversation that occurred with my parents.

Before first grade, as we were driving, my mom said, "Jeff, honey, you are going to a different school next year." This was entirely bizarre to me, as I lived across the street from an outstanding school where my friends from the swim team went. "How come?" I asked. My mom answered, "There is nothing wrong with you, but you are attending a special day class at a different school."

Further, my dad said, "You need some help with reading. Again, nothing is wrong with you; you need some help.

You are very smart." I didn't understand then, and they assured me I was an okay kid. I clung to this reasoning, even though I didn't know why I was attending a different school.

I was a seven-year-old kid who learned I would not be going to school across the street with my friends. Although I didn't know what would change exactly, I was upset. This change brought out my anxiety in new ways I had never experienced before. Would I meet new friends? Would my new teacher be friendly? What about the big kids? Would they pick on me? My perspective about school and the future changed as I experienced fear and anxiety.

To combat my nervousness surrounding the change, my parents signed me up for a recreational baseball team, mostly made up of kids from my new school. The team consisted of seven- and eight-year-olds. I remember attending the first practice and seeing those kids on the field. They all knew each other. They were big, and my mind saw them as bullies. I was petrified. I attached myself to my dad's legs and held on for dear life. I don't believe I ever got on the field and did not continue with that baseball team. Unfortunately, this added to my anxiety.

Chapter Two

Special Needs

Instead of walking across the street to attend school, I had to take a bus. The best part about taking the bus to my new school was that I got picked up at the junior high school parking lot, next to the cafeteria. The cafeteria made the school lunches and snacks, and it just so happened that I waited for the bus when the cookies came out of the oven.

I followed the wonderful smell of fresh-baked cookies into the cafeteria one morning. "Hello, young man, would you like a cookie?" a nice lady said. "Yes, please." They gave me a warm cookie on a sheet of wax paper and encouraged me to visit them whenever I wanted another. The warm peanut butter cookie melted in my mouth. It was heaven. Sure enough, I wandered in the next day and got another cookie. Eventually, they told me the cookies cost money and that I should be prepared to purchase them.

Before my solo wait at the bus stop, I'd slip into the kitchen's back door for a ten-cent treat each day– a hot peanut butter cookie or snickerdoodle, neatly wrapped in wax paper. Often, the cookies would be fresh out of the oven, hot and steaming when I arrived. I devoured the cookies while waiting for the bus ride on the curb. They seemed huge and were as big as my hand. This would start a lifelong love of cookies, especially those still warm from the oven.

While waiting for my cookie one morning, I was mesmer-ized by the impressive mixers and blenders. "See, this is how we mix the cookies, and this is how we bake them," the cafeteria workers explained. I loved the peanut butter cookies so much that I asked them for the recipe. They obliged, and I took it home to my mom. I remember my mom reading the recipe, laughing: "Twenty-five pounds flour, one dozen eggs…" Sometimes, I wonder why I didn't become a baker for a living. (For the record, my mom made excellent peanut butter cookies.)

My new school was a small elementary school with a special day class. On my first day, I understood the situ-ation's levity. There were fewer than a dozen students of differing abilities in my class—some in wheelchairs, some clearly with exceptional needs, and some that looked like normal kids, just like me. This special needs day class was my home for the next three years. I had a lot of one-on-one attention and individual instruction. What I remember most were flashcards. Every day, I worked with a teacher, pronouncing words from flashcards. I remember the teachers were very nice to me.

At the beginning of each day, all the classes would line up on the playground before starting, and I would assemble with my special day class. It soon became clear to other kids at the school that I attended a class with disabled children, and the students continually teased me. For three years, the other kids on the playground teased me, causing significant damage to my self-worth. It started in the morning when all the students had to line up for their class in rows. "You're a retard," they would spit. "You are so dumb you have to go with the retards." They called me "Geoffrey the Giraffe" or "redhead" a lot, but that was nothing like insulting my intelligence.

My loving parents clearly understood what was happening, as they routinely would explain that I was not stupid, just different. They assured me I was fine, and it helped me to survive the daily barrage of insults on the playground. My mom and dad were self-esteem heroes, filling my mind with positive thoughts. Nevertheless, you begin believing it when you are called stupid for a long time. Several students relentlessly teased me, and I could stop it with my fists. Other students in my class could not do this, and I also remember defending them. The playground can be a great place to release energy and spend time outdoors, but it can also be cruel. This name-calling, poor test-taking abilities, and low grades would stay with me for decades. My self-esteem was forever damaged on the playground, and this changed the course of my life.

As a participant in the Cub Scouts program under the Boy Scouts of America, I engaged with a local troop alongside neighborhood kids. Our activities included outdoor adventures like camping, hiking, and backpacking. The program's focus extended beyond the outdoors, emphasizing character development, leadership, and physical fitness, complemented by earning badges through various challenges.

Though I don't recall thoroughly enjoying the experience, I recognize its positive impact on my character development. Following Cub Scouts, the next phase was Webelos, a short transitional stage preparing us for the significant leap to Boy Scouts. In Boy Scouts, the challenges intensified, involving more badges and service projects, with the ultimate goal being the prestigious Eagle badge—a symbol of exemplary leadership qualities.

However, during the Webelos phase, I faced a hurdle. The requirement to memorize speeches proved challenging for me. Despite recognizing the program's benefits, the difficulty with memorization led me to discontinue Webelos, and as a result, I did not progress to Boy Scouts.

Chapter Three

Normal Class

I was sent to a third-grade class part-time to assimilate into the regular classroom. I would attend specific times of the day and then head back to the special day classroom on a schedule. I don't remember much about the class, except for this one older kid who would taunt the class every day with—yes, this is true—cookies. The side of the classroom facing the corridor had windows from the waist up. Somehow, this kid would get out of class and purchase a cookie (can you blame him?). He would walk by our classroom, waving the cookie in front of all of us during class, usually when the poor teacher was trying to teach us something important. I would hear him humming, "YUM," as he slowly slid by. He would rub his belly, smile, and wave the cookie at us. I imagine he would do this to every classroom he passed until he got to his sixth-grade room at the end of the hallway. I remember once, my teacher got so frustrated that he burst out of the classroom to confront the kid. The teacher got in the student's face, causing the kid to back up against the windows. I saw the teacher waving his finger at him, admonishing him for disrupting the class. The only problem was that the teacher failed to confiscate the cookie, and the kid was waving the cookie behind his back for all of us in the classroom to see while enduring the lecture. I will never forget it.

Fourth grade was a new beginning. I could attend the school directly across the street from our house, and I was in a class with many neighborhood friends and an excellent teacher. I had clearly missed some topics in the second and third grades. For example, I needed to improve my knowledge of geography. This year, a new boy named Bill moved several houses away. This was a time of great neighborhood exploration, as Bill and I spent daylight exploring local creeks within walking distance. We would capture tadpoles, fish, frogs, and anything we could get our hands on. Unlike my friends, I was immune to poison oak and never experienced an outbreak of the rash. My friends would show up the next day, itching and scratching their arms. Sports were a popular pastime, including soccer, basketball, baseball, swimming, and tennis during the summer.

Summer days were filled with play and little structure. The creek beside the swimming pool provided hours of exploration, especially on hot summer days. The dense shade and creek bed cooled us off quickly. Thickets of blackberry bushes surrounded the swimming pool, and we visited these all summer. Each summer, we created trails through the blackberries; the best, most ripe berries would be just out of reach. We had to smash the branches down with a board to reach them. I would get scrapes all over my arms and legs, and my hands and shirt would be purple. Almost nothing tastes better than a fresh, ripe blackberry warmed in the sun—except maybe a fresh-baked cookie.

The rest of my elementary school time was less traumatic. I don't know what the teachers were doing to accommodate me. Although I was unaware of my academic struggles, I continued to be pulled from class and sent to a different room for support, mainly related to reading. I remember lots of flashcards and practice with pronunciation. I was in no way made to feel stupid by my fellow students, as my disability was unknown to most. People with dyslexia are known to struggle with rote memorization tasks, and I experienced difficulty in this regard. The months of the year, multiplication tables, and even the alphabet continued to challenge me, as there was no context or experience to commit these things to memory. I excelled athletically and enjoyed recess, physical education, and just being outside.

We could bring our lunch or order lunch through the school district, and there were two ordered meals I relished. The first was Salisbury steak. It would come with gravy and mashed potatoes. The other meal I never missed was pizza. It would come wrapped in aluminum foil, and I would order two. I used to save the aluminum foil and make a ball. I would put it inside my desk and add to it each week, trying to get a larger and larger ball. The aluminum ball would suddenly disappear as soon as it got nice and large. I later discovered that the teacher removed it when it started stinking. That was too bad. I wanted to make the world's most giant aluminum foil ball.

There seemed to be endless time when I was a child. While many children became bored, this was seldom a problem for me. I had so many hobbies and interests that I could jump from one to the other anytime. I was very fond of Fischertechnik, a German toy that encouraged the exploration and building of structures and machinery mechanisms. I would spend hours building table-sized objects. Another hobby was the construction of forts in the backyard. This became a considerable pastime, particularly with my friend Bill. In the 1970s, one could quickly salvage nails and discarded wood from construction sites. It was as simple as going to the discard pile and dragging the item home. We could also visit our garages or the dumpsters at the school across the street for wood, carpet, and even insulation. We constructed forts in my backyard with carpeting, waterproof roofs, locking doors, and battery-operated lighting. Expansions and complete tear-downs and rebuilds occurred. Wood was re-used so much light would shine through the nail holes. After settling in the most recently constructed fort for a few months, I would make a plan for the following structure. I usually tore things apart and started on the new fort myself. Then, I would explain to Bill that there was a new plan. He must have thought I was crazy, but he would join in. The last fort built was three stories high, with carpeting and a flag. This was an escape from life, an escape from school. I was just a kid and did not think about why I enjoyed creating these structures in the backyard. I did not know it then, but this activity was likely a manifestation of a common dyslexic desire to build things.

I was on the summer swim team mostly because everyone else was. I wasn't particularly good at swimming and always felt cold at swim practice. My lips would turn purple, and I would shake while I was in the water. My sister was more of a natural swimmer. However, the swim team was still a lot of fun. I remember sneaking out the night before swim meets with rival teams and doing things to their pool. It would typically consist of decorating their pool with toilet paper. We would attend movies together as a team, go to water parks, and have potlucks. I mingled with kids of all ages and often looked up to the older kids.

I also had a paper route I shared with a friend. We delivered the *Oakland Tribune* seven days a week. We delivered afternoons during the week and mornings on weekends on our bicycles. We used to bundle papers with a rubber band and carry them in a shoulder satchel. We prided ourselves in placing the paper on the doormat. Not only that, but we didn't throw the papers while we rode by on our bicycles. The *Oakland Tribune* produced a thick Sunday paper, and we typically had to take multiple trips. Our route included the steepest street in the neighborhood. We usually rode our bicycles halfway up the hill and then walked. Or better yet, we got our parents to drive us on Sundays.

Chapter Four

Passion Born

When I was nine years old, I won a goldfish in a bag during the cakewalk at the school carnival. Little did I know that was the start of a lifelong passion and career. I took the fish home and put it in a bowl. I was fascinated by the little goldfish. I had been harassing tadpoles and small fish in creeks near the house, but I had yet to get a good view of a fish in clear water. Likewise, I was amazed by how the fish navigated through the water so smoothly and at the function of its fins, design, and, of course, its ability to breathe underwater. Shortly after, I purchased several dozen goldfish and put them in a new fishbowl. The more, the merrier, right? Engrained in my memory is the image of those goldfish swimming in the bowl on top of the dresser in my bedroom.

The next day, some goldfish began to die, and I had a smelly mess on my hands. I had to eliminate the dead fish and figure out what I was doing wrong. A local store called the Glass Bottom Boat was located in downtown Lafayette for many years. The great thing about it was that I could ride my bike there in less than thirty minutes. I proceeded to Glass Bottom Boat with Bill, where we became convinced we needed aquariums.

Bill and I decided to purchase two complete twenty-gallon aquariums. Our parents were supportive as this was thought to be a healthy hobby. Besides, "This is just a phase," Bill's mom said to my mom. Little did she know. It was, in fact, a phase for Bill but not for me! Many children with dyslexia are known to connect with nature, and my curiosity and interest in fish are consistent with these findings.

Despite what Bill's mom thought, my tropical fish-keeping hobby continued to grow. My weekends were filled with fish-related activities, including cleaning my aquariums and riding my bike to nearby towns to look at fish stores. Bill and I would spend an entire day going from store to store. In the 1970s and 1980s, there were a few tropical fish-keeping stores near my house. These stores were very different from today's, where all the tanks are used solely to sell fish in mass quantities. All the stores had the same musty algae-like smell; I got excited just walking into the stores. Suppliers delivered fish on a schedule; I learned the schedule to see the latest imports. I also learned that the best fish were acquired from other hobbyists who returned them if they left the hobby or if the fish got too big. When we purchased fish, the bags would go in our backpacks, and we would ride home with them. I supported my hobby by mowing lawns in the neighborhood. I had several regular clients I would visit on specific days.

I also spent a considerable amount of my time reading aquarium fish books and magazines. Hobbyist books were often broken apart by fish type, care suggestions, plants, etc.; they had plenty of figures and photographs. I learned the fish vocabulary quickly, and I retained it. I would memorize hundreds of Latin fish names, often repeating them as I walked through the house. It was another refuge from school where I could learn and excel. Despite my reading processing difficulties, I was getting something out of the fish books and magazines.

Chapter Five

Oh, this is Difficult

Attending middle school in Lafayette, approximately three miles from home, provided various commuting options. Buses, carpools, bikes, and skateboards were all in play. Engaging with diverse teachers in different subjects daily marked my transition to a larger academic pond. We were getting grades now, and everyone would share how they were doing. My friend would proudly explain, "That was an easy test; I got an A." This reminded me I was limited academically in some manner. That test that he just got an A on? I studied for hours and got a D. I became very confused by the grades I received on multiple-choice tests. I appeared to perform far better with essay responses and in math. My grades didn't seem to match my study efforts. I experienced growing frustration and worry as test anxiety began to affect me. Why was I studying for hours every night only to fail a test? Why all the effort for a C or a D in the class?

I had to work harder than most. I was in survival mode and not thinking about the future.

My difficulty recalling basic information was starting to show. As a typical dyslexic individual, I was pretty good at recalling memories surrounding personal experiences and events close to me. For example, I memorized fish names and details, mainly fish I had in aquariums. Like a vault, my brain stored that information for long periods and could retrieve it quickly. However, basic memorization of facts that were separate from my experience, known as semantic memories, was challenging to keep in my head and retrieve.

I had a physical education teacher who would start every class by discussing the professional baseball stats. He would spout players, teams, and stats, showing his proficiency in semantic topics. One day, I had to deliver something to his class for a teacher. I walked in with the materials, and he was in front of the class. He looked at me and said, "McLain, give me three baseball teams. Any three." In front of the entire class. I could not remember a single team at the time. I was frozen and highly embarrassed.

Some classes, such as woodworking, were far easier than others. I recall my first day of woodworking class. I immediately sat down with my friends, eager to learn. There were pencils on the table and holes in the corners to attach tools, such as vices. I grabbed a pencil and proceeded to shoot it through the hole. The pencil would fly up from the desk in front of my face, and I would catch it and then repeat. The first thing the teacher said as he introduced himself while looking straight at me was, "No playing rocket."

I remember being driven to a learning specialist in Lafayette following middle school several days a week. A family in the neighborhood also had a student going to the learning specialist, and we carpooled. It's funny. I remember the carpool and the drop-off, but there was not much about what was done at the learning specialist other than lots and lots of flashcards. They would hold up flashcards for me, and I would recite the words. I didn't understand the purpose of the flashcards at the time. Still, I now believe the repetition and pronunciation of words addressed my learning disability by working with my text-to-sound abilities.

I was a very skinny kid and was conscious of it. I was also unusually fast and was on the traveling soccer team with students from the area, some of whom were at my school. Our coach was the best coach ever, and I had him for several years. Supportive and friendly, he just loved the game of soccer. I also played soccer in junior high and tried out for football. I was well below the weight limit to make the A-team for football, but they made an exception due to my speed. In the first game in Walnut Creek, I was knocked on my behind after every play by a much larger kid from the opposite team. He was friendly, but

I had no chance. I remember he would give me blocking tips as he helped me up from the ground. "Get your arms up," and "Keep your feet shoulder-width apart," he would suggest. It was then that I realized football was probably not for me! I stopped playing the next day, claiming I had "too much homework." In my case, this was probably true.

I was asked to be a teacher's aide for the physical education class, making for a second outdoor class in eighth grade. I loved that class! I was able to demonstrate sports activities, referee games, and more. The teacher was impressive; he knew how to play just about every sport and had muscles bulging through his clothes.

I made more fish friends in middle school and mostly continued to keep a type of tropical fish called cichlids. Cichlids are egg-laying fish with sophisticated behaviors, striking colors, and aggressive attitudes. One of my new friends was interested in Siamese fighting fish, also called bettas. Male bettas were notorious for fighting to the death. This is why they are always sold separately. They make excellent beginner fish, as they gulp air from the surface, allowing them to be kept in tiny containers. My friend started a routine fish fight during lunch. We would bring our bettas in containers, put them together, and take wagers!

My family began attending an Episcopal church called St. Stephen's in the hills of Orinda. We were invited by families and friends from the swim club. It became a Sunday morning routine. I was not overly excited to attend at first, but I enjoyed the stop for donuts on the way home. Soon, I became more involved and began to enjoy it. I decided to get confirmed at thirteen, committing to Jesus Christ and receiving the Holy Spirit through the bishop's laying of hands. I attended confirmation classes at St. Stephen's and was confirmed by Bishop Swing in San Francisco on a beautiful day in April 1981. I remember many parts of that day, and I still have my Book of Common Prayer, signed by the bishop. It was a great feeling to be part of a church. I became an acolyte and enjoyed participating in Sunday services with the priests. I was also paid to help at weddings. I got to sit up front with the priests, who were exceptionally nice guys. I am thankful for the seeds of faith planted by my parents and St. Stephen's. Although I wouldn't see the fruits of those seeds for decades, their impact was immense.

Chapter Six

High School

I was nervous about starting high school. High school was more extensive and likely more challenging than junior high school, and I was stressed about the difficulty I would experience academically. Then, I discovered weightlifting. As a skinny person, I was interested in getting stronger and bigger. I became inspired by Arnold Schwarzenegger's bodybuilding autobiography, *Arnold: The Education of a Bodybuilder*. My afternoons and evenings were filled with soccer, weightlifting, and running. When I started driving, I joined gyms and spent evenings lifting weights. Thinking back to this, I believe this was an attempt to compensate for my learning disability and low self-esteem. If I couldn't excel in the classroom, perhaps I could excel in the weight room. This kept me away from the wrong crowd and, in addition, helped repair my self-esteem.

I attended Campolindo, one of the state's most presti-gious and rigorous public high schools. Academics were challenging, and good grades and college pressures were real. The teachers frequently gave students mul-tiple-choice tests, which I often failed. I was particularly frustrated with my results, as I usually knew the answers. I discovered that I seemed to misread test questions. I knew the information, but my test results would not show it. I realized this when going back over the exams with teachers and others. Double negatives in test questions were especially difficult for me. For example, I would miss the word "not" or "won't" in the question and the potential answer choices. Not only was I misinterpreting the question, but I was also misinterpreting the possible answer choices. Students with dyslexia need contextual clues to answer multiple-choice questions successfully. A specific test question on a multiple-choice test is often a detailed and particular request with a lack of overall context, making things difficult for me. I also continued to exhibit other symptoms of dyslexia, such as trouble reading certain words and problems with names and dates. I knew something was wrong, but I didn't think it was dyslexia. The scars from my childhood remained, and I thought I was "stupid." I was barely maintaining a C average.

One class was particularly tough for me—Spanish with Ms. Danielle. Ms. Danielle was known for being a chal-lenging teacher, and many avoided her during their high school years. I probably spent as much time studying for Spanish as all my other classes combined to maintain a grade of a C. Ms. Danielle was aware of my challenges and remained patient and accommodating. However, she wasn't particularly pleased when I had to leave early for track meets. Several times a year, I was one of just a few select people who moved beyond the regular track season, and I would have to tell her I wouldn't be present in class. She would reprimand me, saying, "Oh, Jefe... oh, Jefe." However, I had to work with her and learn to use my homework time efficiently. I even signed up for a second year of Spanish with Ms. Danielle, and it was not until well after high school that I understood she was a lifesaver. Because of her class, I learned to study and use my time wisely. These lessons were transferable to college. Ms. Danielle was a strict teacher with a bad reputation among many other students, but she cared. Heroes like Ms. Danielle were placed in my path throughout my lifetime, and I am forever thankful for them.

I frequently visited the Steinhart Aquarium in Golden Gate Park, San Francisco, seeking fish inspiration. I would convince my mom to take me to the aquarium, and I would wander around in amazement, naming all the fish and just staring at them. The Steinhart Aquarium was an excellent public aquarium with hundreds of species across dozens of separate exhibits and biotopes, with a giant freshwater fish section and several aquariums focusing on cichlids. Looking at the large aquariums made me want to expand my personal aquarium collection, and I continued to purchase aquariums, some up to one hundred gallons in capacity. I had approximately ten aquariums in my little room, so my dad moved me to the spare bedroom, which was larger. He also constructed stands for me. I must have driven him crazy. I would walk down the hall with buckets of water weekly as I performed water changes and maintenance. I also took advantage of his being at work during the day to bring new aquariums. When my dad asked if my aquarium was new, I used to say it wasn't brand new and that I'd had it for a while. Eventually, he caught on to my tricks.

One of the soccer parents was a cichlid enthusiast, and we connected, resulting in a great friendship. I took care of his aquariums when his family traveled, and he introduced me to the American Cichlid Association, a group that shares information about cichlids. They hold conferences across the United States and have local chapters that have fish auctions and meetings. Auctions were a great place to get rare fish. Costly fish found in stores were $10 or $20 each at auction. I would get rides from my fish friend to these auctions in San Jose, and I could bid on several of my favorite types of fish. This was such a great experience. He also gave me his entire collection of *Buntbarsch Bulletins*, the American Cichlid Association's monthly journal. It contained articles about cichlid keeping, and I used to pull them out and read through them frequently.

I love sharing my best practical joke with my kids, even though they're probably tired of it by now. Now, you get to hear it. First, I must explain the situation in the high school library that I had to endure for several years. I often went to the library before the day's first period to study. I was almost always distracted by the noisy cheerleaders who would commandeer the large conference table in front of the library. Their continuous screeching, talking, laughing, and disrespectful behavior was highly annoying. I guess these girls didn't need to study like I did.

Bill's family had a mouse infestation in their garage, and we would practice our mouse-catching skills. We finally captured one, and I put it in a coffee can and brought it to school. I had no specific plans for the mouse; I wanted to release it somewhere. Sitting in the library with the coffee can in front of me, I had a thought. Would they even notice if I let this mouse go near those rude cheerleaders? It was a stretch, but I gave it a shot. I let the mouse out of the coffee can where I was sitting. Behold, it proceeded directly to the cheerleaders and quickly skittered under the table as they were gossiping. Immediately, one of them shouted, "EW, A MOUSE!" and the next screamed, and the next screamed, and so on. Nearly every one of them stood on their chairs as they screamed. It couldn't have been better. The librarian quickly caught the mouse by the tail and released it outside. This was, perhaps, my best prank ever.

I blew off steam by playing basketball at the school across the street. It was my large playground, and I would head outside with a basketball at random times just to shoot and think. Bill would often meet me there. We would play basketball, soccer, tennis, and other sports. The school was typically desolate on weekends, so we had a large playground.

We were familiar with every part of the school, including the roof. We knew how to get up to the roof in various places. We would repeatedly walk around on the roof just because we could. We frequently kicked balls onto the roof and had to retrieve them. Once, I kicked a basketball onto the roof. I went to get it as Bill continued to shoot baskets. I searched on the roof for the basketball and couldn't find it. On my way back, I looked down into a courtyard and saw the basketball. In a split second, I jumped off the roof to grab it. As I was leaning down to get positioned to jump off the roof, I slipped and fell headfirst. I put my right arm out to break my fall and *crack*—I broke my wrist. I quickly snapped it back into place with my adrenaline. I grabbed the ball and went back to shoot baskets.

As I was walking, it became clear that my wrist was still broken. It started to hurt a lot, and I began to see stars and black and white. I quickly sat on a bench by the basketball hoops. Bill came over and said, "Are you okay? You look pale." I then told him the story. He walked me home, and my dad took me to the emergency room, where the doctor adjusted my wrist again and put it in a cast for six weeks.

In high school, I discontinued soccer to focus on track and field. In my sophomore year, I made the varsity team and was on the 1600-meter relay with three seniors. It was the time of my life! We would get so pumped up before our races. I was a young kid, and they were very encouraging. I excelled in the 400-meter sprint and 300-meter hurdles and made great friends on the track team.

During my junior year, my friend Vince and I were very successful in the hurdles and secured the top two spots in the league. Vince was a year older than me and the only Black person in our school. One day, after we finished our run in the neighborhood surrounding our school, someone called the police to report a "Black man" running. This incident shed light on what type of neighborhood I lived in.

When he graduated, I went on to be undefeated in the hurdles my senior year. My sports idol was Edwin Moses, a famous 400-meter hurdler who held the world record and was undefeated for ten incredible years.

My favorite track coach was a former track star and professional football player. He lived in Oakland, and I was very fond of him. He always treated me fairly and was highly knowledgeable. He would stay late and work on my hurdling after the regular workouts. Halfway through my senior year, my favorite coach stopped coming, and there were rumors he got fired. I was devastated and had to finish my senior year without him. I never found out why he was fired.

I started to experience a recurring nightmare in high school that would hit me several nights a week. I would be in the front seat of a car, sometimes behind the wheel, and sometimes in the passenger seat. I would drive up a hill that got steeper and steeper as I went. As I continued, the hill became a mountain, like I was at the top of the world. It got extremely steep as I approached the top and felt like I would fall backward. This is precisely when I would wake up. I never reached the top of the mountain. I wouldn't find out until years later what it was about.

Unfortunately, my GPA was just above 2.0, and I needed more than academics to get into college. Then, there was the Standardized Assessment Test, otherwise known as the SAT, the monster of all multiple-choice tests. Like a cow led to the slaughter, I took the SAT with the rest of the students, but I stayed quiet when they talked about their scores. I don't remember my exact score—I think I removed my score from my memory, as it was so embarrassing. My SAT scores were so poor that they provided little assistance in gaining acceptance to college. I graduated from high school in 1985.

Chapter Seven

Sonoma State University

I was interested in attending college close to home and running on a track team. I toured Sonoma State University with the track coach and was persuaded to apply, as they were set for a new track and were building the team. I applied to Sonoma State University and California State University, Chico. I got accepted to Sonoma State but with a condition. I was accepted into an Equal Opportunity Program called Summer Bridge. Summer Bridge's goals were to provide self-confidence and create a sense of community for academically disadvantaged incoming students. I don't recall knowing I was a part of this program until the summer I was to report to Sonoma State. Unbeknownst to me, I was also accepted through the Disability Resource Center. I had to show up at Sonoma State before the incoming freshman class. I stayed in the dorms, took reading and math classes, and got to know many other students in the program to help acclimate me. I made friends that would last my entire college career and beyond. This program instilled self-confidence and helped me transition to college.

At first, I found college easier than my demanding high school. This surprised me. I observed others in the Summer Bridge program struggling with introductory coursework, yet I was somewhat excited I was doing better than most. Likewise, I participated in track the first year and found it rewarding. My times were slower than my high school times, and I was not winning all my races, which was hard to swallow. I was unable to improve my times that first year. Much of that is because I focused on weightlifting, which I enjoyed more. I became friends with the track team's strength coach, a doctorate student at Sonoma State. He was an avid powerlifter and Olympic weightlifter. He introduced me to powerlifting, and I was hooked. During my second year, I decided to drop track and pursue competitive powerlifting instead, as the two sports did not complement each other.

I would work out most days in the Sonoma State gym with the strength coach, a few other diehards, and some football team members. The strength coach had keys to the gym and training room, which was excellent. He lived with his wife nearby, and he would often use my computer to type essays, and I would drive him home.

The strength coach convinced me to enter powerlifting meets to set goals and improve my lifting.

I remember one guy named Kent from the gym at Sonoma State. He was a community member and was always working out. He had arms the size of my legs and tried out every year for the Oakland Raiders. He appeared very intimidating, and I didn't talk to him for at least a year. While waiting to get into the gym, we started talking one day. What a nice guy! We ended up talking a lot after that. I could always start a conversation with him by asking about his bench press. "How did you get your bench press so strong?" He would reply with thought, "It is all about triceps; you have to have powerful arms for the bench press."

During my sophomore year, the strength coach recruited a legitimate powerlifter. This guy was a monster. He had legs the size of tree trunks and would squat upwards of 700 pounds with flawless form. He helped all of us learn and improve our lifts. Occasionally, he would get upset if he missed a lift and start throwing things and punching the walls. Fortunately, the walls were padded!

I enjoyed the powerlifting scene and became aware that many powerlifters were on steroids. I had decided early in my life to avoid all steroids, smoking, and illegal substances. Having successfully competed in several contests in the area and enjoying the continuous challenge of lifting heavier and heavier weights, I started to enter more significant powerlifting competitions. I won the entire competition at a meet in Santa Rosa, California, and my days competing in novice competitions were over. I was required to compete in an "open" contest, which included professional powerlifters. I entered an open competition in San Jose, California, and didn't even make the podium in my weight class. There were lifters far above my ability, and I became very discouraged. For example, while my best squat was 445 pounds, a guy was squatting over 600 pounds in my weight class.

It wasn't long after this that one of my workout partners at the gym offered me steroids. I asked some questions and was polite, but ultimately, I said no. This person found an aspiring weightlifter interested in taking steroids, and I witnessed a complete transformation of this guy in the gym. His bench press nearly doubled to more than 400 pounds over two months. Then, suddenly, he shrunk back to his usual self after stopping the steroids. I have no regrets about skipping the steroids; it was never in my genes to take shortcuts.

I befriended Nick, one of the football players who was much larger than me and shared the desire to lift heavy weights and compete. We spent a lot of time in the gym as lifting partners for a year. He always wanted to play heavy metal or punk rock in the gym while we worked out. People would complain, and he would tell them to shut up and leave if they didn't like it!

I no longer got priority class registration through the track team but was able to get it through the Disability Resource Center. They asked for my help with the flow and organization of students during registration, and I gladly accepted. The individuals in this department were a pleasure to work with, particularly diligent and competent. They were always there to help me and offer advice. Janis, one of my advisors, used a wheelchair and had no arms. She typed, talked on the phone, and did all her work using a device in her mouth. It had a little red thing on the end of a stick that looked like an eraser. I was mesmerized, watching her efficiently do her work with no arms. Janis and the other staff at the Disability Resource Center enlightened me about the capabilities of individuals with disabilities, demonstrating that they can contribute significantly to meaningful work and deserve recognition.

I needed to determine a major soon. My first degree of choice was kinesiology until the courses scared me off. Memorizing muscles, tendons, and body parts made me gasp. Then, I pursued computer science. I took computer programming in high school and performed well in the course. Besides, computer science people made lots of money, so this was a good choice. This phase lasted longer than the kinesiology phase. I took basic computer programming in the second semester of my freshman year and did well; however, I spent five or more hours a day on homework. I received a B+ in computer programming, which was better than most classes. Still, I was skeptical that I could handle the time commitment of several computer classes in one semester.

In my sophomore year, I took biology and was in the same class as my roommate, an English major. I recall him complaining about the rigors of biology and how much time it took to study. I enjoyed studying biology as it came naturally and was not too stressful. I survived with a C+ despite the professor's heavy use of multiple-choice tests and decided to investigate the field of biology further. It was zoology next. Zoology was a ruthless class, covering a dizzying amount of information that demanded a lot of flashcards and studying. While studying zoology, I faced many difficulties due to the heavy workload and challenging tests. However, I was fortunate enough to have Dr. Brumbagh as my professor. He was incredibly supportive, patient, and understanding, which helped me get through the tough times. We would review my exam results together, and he would point out where I made mistakes, even when I knew the correct answers. Thanks to his guidance, he quickly became my favorite teacher and my advisor.

To level the playing field, I was allowed to take tests without time limits. To arrange for disability accommodations, it is necessary to contact the disability department and the professor beforehand. Most professors were very understanding and accommodating, but my results showed only slight improvement when making these special arrangements. When I looked at a complicated multiple-choice test question lacking context, I could read it twice or twenty times, but it didn't make a difference. I couldn't understand it.

After surviving zoology and completing chemistry with a B, I decided to pursue biology. I changed my major to Aquatic Biology with a marine emphasis. I quickly became interested in marine invertebrates and was fascinated with the intertidal marine life environment. My favorite course was Functional Morphology of Marine Invertebrates. In this two-part graduate course, we would travel to the tide pools, collect invertebrates, and bring them back nearly every week. We would study our collections the following week and return them to the beach on the next trip. There were no multiple-choice tests in this class, and concepts were often demonstrated with visual sketches and diagrams rather than narratives, which suited my learning style well. Finals were all oral, and students would get called on random topics about marine invertebrates. This was an excellent learning environment for me.

Bodega Bay was just forty-five minutes from campus, and not only did we go frequently for marine biology, but I would drive to the beach with my friends on a whim. The beaches just north of Bodega Bay were semi-exposed, and each was a unique beach with a parking lot and trail down to the water. Some beaches were composed of sand, some had pea-sized gravel, and some had giant boulders with crashing waves. My favorite was Portuguese Beach, with its pea-sized gravel. I remember just lying there listening to the waves, talking with my friends. Sometimes, we would leave for the beach late on a Friday night, hang out, and talk with the waves crashing until the early morning hours. How I wish I could go back to that time in my life!

Learning about ancestral and primitive invertebrate parts interested me in evolution, and I read books on the topic. My favorite author at the time was Stephen Jay Gould, a famous American author who wrote about evolutionary biology. Gould romanticized evolution, and I was hooked. His powerful and influential books include *Mismeasure of Man*, which investigates and questions craniometry (a measure of brain size) and its relation to intelligence, and *The Panda's Thumb*, which contains information and opinions on natural history. Gould didn't seem interested in finding dual interpretations of evolution and religion. He was often controversial and a dangerous read for an impressionable college student.

I say dangerous because I had believed in God my entire life, and even during college, I continued to pray frequently. I hadn't attended church since late high school, but my memories of St. Stephen's were always with me. The study of marine biology and reading Stephen Jay

Gould was driving a wedge in my head between religion and science. I began to start thinking scientists had all the answers and religion was not based on fact, history, and reality. My favorite book by Gould was *Wonderful Life*, a book about the explosion of aquatic life found in the fossil record in the Burgess Shale of Canada. Gould hypothesized a rapid evolutionary event with many experimental animals as if evolution was trying out various animal types. He hypothesized that many new types of animals were present for multiple reasons, such as mutations and unknown transition animals. Many organisms didn't make it, but some did. I thoroughly enjoyed the newly documented animals sketched in the book that appeared to be from outer space.

Gould could not explain that there is no known mechanism for animals to appear through a mutation process. There are so many gaps explaining transitions that his hypothesis was highly unlikely. His fancy terminology, such as "punctuated equilibrium," romanticized the issue, put a term on it, and made it seem possible. Gould published *Wonderful Life* thirty years ago, and scientists continue to observe tremendous gaps in the fossil record—yet they have an abundance of fossils. The evidence of evolution that Gould was presenting wasn't there. In science, hypotheses are tested and investigated to confirm their claim. Gould appeared to show a bunch of untested hypotheses. Few such hypotheses can be or have been tried; thus, his ideas have not been proven right or wrong. They continue to be just that—ideas. Where is the evidence of evolution? I started to weigh the evidence of evolution and the evidence of God. I was beginning to realize it took far more faith for me to believe in evolution than to believe in God.

Then, there was my paleontology course. I took the class with geologists, and I "rocked" it! My invertebrate morphology courses enabled me to identify and name many fossils and animals.

My roommate was a voracious reader. He was a huge Stephen King fan, and he would tell me about the books. This piqued my interest, and I started reading Stephen King for enjoyment. I could read books at a moderate pace and found a lot of enjoyment in reading. This was the beginning of a lifetime love of reading. I enjoyed literature and English topics in school and could complete the writing assignments with good grades. I could get my thoughts coherently on paper; however, I continued to avoid certain words I could not spell. I never seemed to get the spelling of these words straight in my head. Using words I commonly misspelled would require that I look them up in the dictionary, costing me precious time.

It is my understanding my brain had been compensating for my disability, and I was adjusting in a typical dyslexic fashion. Beginning readers without dyslexia use the left and right sides of the brain to read. In forming readers with dyslexia, the right side of the brain is primarily engaged while reading, and activity is absent from the left side of the brain. With practice, individuals with dyslexia can begin to use both sides of the brain as beginning readers do; however, they continue to rely more on the right side. This compensation phenomenon is understood to be universal among all people with dyslexia, even among different languages. Individuals with dyslexia are known to develop slower than nondyslexic readers and are typically late-bloomers in reading development. Finally, the heavy use of the right side of the brain emphasizes big-picture interpretations and less detail. This explains many challenges I faced with detailed test questions in school.

I was volunteering at the Steinhart Aquarium in San Francisco as a tide pool interpreter. I would put on a microphone and talk about the different tide pool animals, answer questions, and keep unruly field trips full of kids from throwing starfish at each other. This wasn't particularly fun—it was too chaotic for me. "Starfish have little tubes on them that they use to walk and attach to things," I would explain. I would witness a kid throwing a starfish at someone else, and then I would have to say, "We don't throw animals at each other; we respect them." I could hear some classes before I could see them. They would be running down the corridors of the aquarium out of control. Then, other classes would be completely under control. The best part of the entire experience was getting into the aquarium for free once a week.

I would spend most of my time enjoying the aquarium from the public side after my volunteer shifts. I also enjoyed going to the employee entrance and wandering the basement halls. It was dimly lit and chilly down there but filled with surprises. I would pass offices and labs with fish in aquariums, microscopes, and various equipment. All these people were in white lab coats. Once, I toured the preserved fish collection, one of the most populous in the world. I even touched a famous and extremely rare fish called a coelacanth. Coelacanths existed more than 360 million years ago and were thought to be extinct until one was discovered in 1938. This was a fantastic experience for a fish guy, leaving me smiling for weeks. Another time, I was walking through the basement and smelled a powerful odor of fish and marine birds. As I turned the corner, a dozen penguins were hanging out on rocks before me. I said hello and continued on my way.

I started working for an aquarium store in Rohnert Park part way through college. This was a great way to earn extra money and feed my demanding hobby. A sweet elderly lady had purchased the store for her grandchildren, a young man and a woman. Unfortunately, the grandson was highly unreliable and, in addition, would enter the store from time to time, grab all the money in the till, and leave. The granddaughter oversaw the funds and operations and could not control the continual theft. The grandma was nice and confided in me that some things were happening with the grandson. I was reliable and opened and closed the store without any issues.

We always used to keep the register key under it, so when I opened it every morning, I grabbed and unlocked the drawer. One morning, I lifted the register to get the key and saw a coiled coral snake, an escapee from the bird and reptile store next door. If there was ever a time for me to get a heart attack from fright, that would have been it.

I enjoyed the interaction with the customers. I was the freshwater fish guy and shared information about fish with them. One customer named Henry would come every week for feeder goldfish. These are cheap goldfish used to feed large predatory fish that demanded live fish food. He had large fish called oscars and would purchase hundreds of feeders every week. We would get into debates about all sorts of things.

One day, Henry asked what my favorite fish was. I promptly said, "The Midas cichlid." He thought about it for a minute. Then he looked at some similar-looking fish at the store called red devils and said, "Those are the same as red devils." "No, they aren't," I replied. He retorted, "Yes, they are the same." This was before the internet and mobile phones, and we could not find the true answer. So, I said, "How about I call the Steinhart Aquarium and ask for the cichlid expert?" He agreed that would settle our disagreement.

I called the Steinhart Aquarium and talked with Frank, the caretaker for the freshwater fish exhibits, who confirmed they were of different species. He explained the difference in the head shape of the two fish species over the phone. There are more than 20,000 types of fish, and it is not uncommon for separate species to look the same at first glance. I won the bet and met a new person at the Steinhart Aquarium. Soon, I began volunteering to help Frank feed and maintain displays after my tide pool task. Frank maintained a large portion of the freshwater fish section of the Steinhart Aquarium at the time, and it contained many cichlids.

I remember my first day helping Frank. He had me wipe the inside walls of an aquarium that housed a sizeable white piranha with huge teeth. Cleaning tanks with piranha and other fish with large teeth always made me nervous. Frank said not to worry, it wouldn't bite me. He recently fed it, and it didn't have a reason to taste a finger. The scary piranha sat in the corner and watched me the entire time. When I was ready to wipe the other side of the aquarium, I just moved to the piranha's side, and it moved to the opposite side for me.

I would often cut up frozen fish into bite-sized chunks and feed the fish for Frank. It was fun feeding them from above. Frank had his favorites, which were mostly the gars. He always ensured I loaded food pieces with vitamins when I fed the gars. I liked cleaning tanks when fish were still in them, swimming around my legs as I carefully wiped things down and siphoned debris.

I was at a Santa Rosa mall with a large aquarium with two giant fish in front of a store. These fish were Midas cichlids, and they were tending a large batch of their babies. Both were peach-colored and the coolest-looking cichlids I had ever seen. The pair I watched were descendants of famous Midas cichlids from the Berlin Aquarium. They were selling babies at the store, and I purchased a group of these fish and raised them in a 55-gallon tank until they got too large for the aquarium. I sold all but the one largest fish of the bunch I affectionately named "Blockhead." He was approximately one foot long, at least eight inches high, and had a large fatty deposit the size of a golf ball on his head. He would follow me back and forth, begging for food when I walked by the aquarium. Blockhead was moved to a 75-gallon tank in 1995. In 1996, I located a female Midas cichlid in Berkeley that I affectionately named Rosey and successfully mated this fish with Blockhead. Blockhead and Rosey had hundreds of babies. After some mating fun, Blockhead was moved to his 180-gallon tank, where he lived the rest of his life. He moved gravel during the day, making pits in the bottom of the tank. I would also hear him moving gravel when I woke up at night. I am not sure that fish ever rested. He lived nine years—a long time for a fish of this type, but not the oldest of my collection. I had a green severum that lived thirteen years.

Because I switched majors too much and took light course loads, I took five years to graduate from a four-year university. One class, ichthyology, caused a delay. Sonoma State claimed they didn't have enough students to fill an ichthyology class, and I got together with several students to petition for a course. It was approved; however, it took time for the school to find a professor. The following year, we had a professor from UC Davis teach us ichthyology—all day on Fridays. This class was a fish person's dream, with field trips capturing live fish, fish identification, and dissection. Each of us was required to find a large fish, remove the flesh, and construct a complete skeleton of the fish. We had to memorize all the bones.

I had my last meeting with my academic advisor, confirming I was to graduate with a degree in aquatic biology. I remember calling my dad and checking in with him. "Have you thought about graduate school?" he asked. "You probably need an advanced degree to be competitive in your field." I hadn't thought much about it, as I mostly thought about my potential career options.

Sometime later, I agreed to apply to graduate school at San Francisco State University in the marine biology department. As I neared graduation, I noticed I was getting a bachelor of arts instead of a bachelor of science in aquatic biology. I was uncertain about the consequences, but it is what it is. I graduated from Sonoma State in 1990 with a bachelor of arts and a grade point average of 2.9.

I don't know how I was accepted at San Francisco State University, but I was accepted, and a new adventure began.

Chapter Eight

San Francisco State University

I started graduate school at San Francisco State University as a commuter from my parents' house in Lafayette. I used the Bay Area Rapid Transit train (BART) to transport me to Daly City. Once in Daly City, I hopped on a bus for a short ride to the university. It was often warm in Lafayette, which was inland, and cold and foggy when I arrived in Daly City, as San Francisco State was close to the Pacific Coast.

My first semester at San Francisco State nearly destroyed me. My physics course was all multiple-choice tests, and I needed help. Worse was systematic biology with one of the worst teachers I'd ever had. I don't think I understood anything. Population biology was exciting and not multiple-choice test-based. I received two Bs and a C, and my ego was rocked. I was on academic probation.

Despite my grade difficulty, San Francisco State was a unique and enjoyable experience. The sun would usually come out around lunchtime, and I would fall asleep on the lawn in the quad. There was always something happening in the quad. They had an open microphone time, and anyone could step up and talk. They just had to follow some basic rules—no profanity, etc. People would walk up to the microphone and talk about something they believed in. I never had the guts to try such a thing, but I liked to listen to the perspective of others. Students also staged protests. Once, protesting students built shacks of plywood and cardboard on the lawn. They lived in the shacks for several weeks, and the school finally got permission to bulldoze them.

I took a two-week trip to Germany with a girlfriend in 1991. She grew up in Germany and was excited to visit relatives and spend time with extended family. We stayed at her grandparents' house in Giessen, a short drive from Frankfurt. Her grandparents didn't speak English, and I didn't speak German. I relied on my girlfriend to translate. I studied up on my German and got comfortable enough to go out on my own and get a beer and bratwurst. There was a cute little shack right outside the home where we were staying that sold fantastic beer. I would go out every day and get a beer. We spent our days visiting relatives, castles, and other historical sites.

Once, we visited friends and talked for a long time in their living room. One of them was a psychologist, and they liked to talk about and interpret dreams. I remember where I was sitting, the large window and couch in front of it. The room had lots of photos and trinkets on the walls. As we shared each other's dreams and talked about them, I got the guts to mention my mountain nightmare dream.

After I described the dream, the woman asked me a few questions. First, she asked what my school situation was like. She then asked about my work situation. Her interpretation of my dream floored me. "Oh, that is simple," she said. "You have not found your career, and that climb up the hill is you searching for your career. That dream will be gone when you find it." It made a lot of sense. I had a troubled educational background, had been in graduate school, and had no idea what I was to do. I am happy to report that my nightmare ceased visiting me when I started working as a biologist.

I returned to San Francisco State to finish my coursework. I had another defining teacher and course—fisheries biology, taught by Dr. Larson, an excellent communicator and teacher. He opened my world to fisheries biology, introducing me to a career I had no idea existed. A job that involved fish. What? I could work with fish and get paid?

My master's thesis was about search image formation of a common cichlid fish. The fundamental mechanism of this learning is thought to be the development of an image, typically the shape of the prey item, that helps the predator find the item quickly. It may be the shape, color pattern, or any other distinguishing characteristic. Birds are known to improve their foraging by repeated exposure to a prey item over time. This is thought to be due to search image formation. Such a phenomenon had never been demonstrated in fish. I selected the convict cichlid, as they are readily available, durable, and visual predators.

Chapter Nine

Acalanes Union High School District

I had a few odd jobs during my youth, including being a dishwasher, warehouse boy, laborer, and landscaper. I worked the longest as a general laborer in the maintenance department of the Acalanes Union High School district. A high school friend told me about this summer job. He was on the painting crew, where they moved from school to school, painting classrooms, hallways, and just about every surface that needed paint. I applied and was hired for summer help for several years while in college at Sonoma State. Somehow, I managed to meet the requirements, so I was invited to stay on year-round. I juggled work alongside my graduate studies at San Francisco State for several years during the school year. What would seem like an ordinary labor job had lots of lessons.

The maintenance department's staff consisted mainly of Vietnam veterans, each with unique experiences and stories to share. Their strong sense of patriotism was admirable, and I respected them for their dedicated service. Recognizing the need to work effectively with my non-typical colleagues, I developed strong relationships with many of them over time. The secret to my success was always to do what I was told.

A guy named Vince was the common laborer, and he would often show up very dirty. He always seemed to have his hands on messy tasks. He would siphon gas using a hose—he would start it with his mouth and spit out the gas when it got in his mouth, and he got the siphon started. He would perform tasks such as recycling, fueling, transportation, etc. There was a very nice side to Vince. He knew of a great burrito place in an inner city part of Oakland and would bring them to us for lunch. Sometimes, he would surprise us. Luke was a contractor, and he chewed tobacco so frequently his driver's door was stained with spit. The gardeners were a fun bunch and always played card games throughout the day (sometimes even during break)! Cussing was expected, and donuts were frequent. Fred was the foreman, and he was very old and wise. He was the peacemaker and often settled disputes and disagreements about work methods. Fred would notice safety violations and stop things before they got out of control. A lot could be learned about diplomacy from Fred. He smoked constantly and only had one lung. Once you knew these men and broke through their exterior, they would give you the shirts off their backs. The painter helped me paint my car one weekend.

I was a general helper and treated as the least important person. Because I was the only temporary employee helping, I got a wide variety of jobs, some enjoyable and some downright horrible. I liked working with the landscapers. Every big thing was done with a machine, so the labor wasn't bad. Digging was infrequent. I remember poisoning gophers in fields for extended periods. We would use these poles with poison on the end. We pushed the pole into the ground and released the poison, which would be underground so birds wouldn't get it. Occasionally, high school students would be on the fields when I poisoned gophers. "What are you doing?" they would ask. Not wanting them to know I was poisoning gophers, I would say, "We are checking for water. All good here."

When I was on the painting crew, we were trying to finish a hallway quickly, and I was rolling up a storm. The big boss came to check out our progress, and my boss was explaining what significant progress we were making. As I diligently painted with a roller in their presence, I stepped right into the paint tray, much to their amusement. It was perfect timing. Fortunately, the person visiting was Fred, and he broke into laughter.

Did you know that roofs needed to be painted? Yes, you paint them, commonly silver. Very steep roofs over gymnasiums and large buildings are often painted with reflective and waterproof paint. How do you do that? You send the temporary help on the roof, tie a rope to his belt, and give him the sprayer. I would get paint all over my shoes and pants and slip in wet paint frequently as I slowly rappelled down roofs, painting simultaneously.

I spent weeks at a time removing the tops of desks and prepping them for staining and reconditioning. It went like this: remove the top of the desk, flip the top over, get a chisel and hammer, and knock off rock-hard bubble gum. Usually, you would try to hit your coworker with the bubble gum. As the smell of grape bubble gum filled the room, we would pile the metal parts in one corner and the desktops in another. This task would last weeks, stretching us to keep boredom at bay.

I did my share of work repairing roofs and carrying heavy buckets of boiling tar up tall ladders. It was a challenging and risky job as I had to be extra cautious to avoid getting burned by the scorching tar while spreading it over the roofs.

When we put in cement, we had to watch it during school hours so the kids wouldn't carve their initials in it. Students would offer me money to let them carve their initials. I always said no. The schools with more well-off students provided the most generous financial incentives. I was once offered $50 for a chance to carve initials in the cement.

Later, they paired me up with a new employee. He was quiet and initially appeared weird. His name was John. After a few weeks of working together, we started talking about where we grew up and came from. Hands shaking, John explained part of his life and said, "I was put in a hole and ate bugs in the war." He said he was tortured and was a prisoner of war for several years. My eyes were opened. To say I was fortunate growing up in the East Bay and attending college was an understatement. This man was severely damaged in a war fighting for our freedom. I felt insignificant and tiny. I wanted to do things for John, but he wasn't ready to talk much. Respect!

One of the high schools had a flea problem. Fleas were biting kids during class. Treating the classrooms did nothing because of the stray cat population that lived in the school's crawl space. The maintenance department poisoned the cats, hoping to solve the problem, but it created a new issue. A very smelly issue.

One day, Fred called a meeting. Not one to mince words, Fred said, "We need to remove a bunch of dead cats from underneath the high school." He explained that we would have all the protection and tools needed, including white hazmat suits, headlamps, and official gas masks. Not believing this was happening, I explained that it was probably a pest control company's job to do such a thing. Yeah, that went over well.

Our task was clear. We needed to go into the crawl space with bags, grab dead cats, put them in the bags, and drag them back out. There were three of us. This was a large school, and it would take several hours of crawling in the dark. As we started our trek, I remember looking at our white hazmat suits covered with little black dots. Fleas. As we crawled from room to room, we would find deceased cats and put them in the bags. They were at various stages of decomposition. Some were dried out completely and just a skeleton with fur, some were bloated, and some had maggots all over them. It was a lot to handle— a full gas mask, a hazmat suit, a headlamp, and a bag of dead cats.

I was second in line at the time, and John was in front of me when he put his hand in the belly of a rotten cat. He yelled, "Found a cat!" We brought the bags out, and they were bloody, smelly messes. I remember taking them to the dumpster and people complaining they smelled terrible.

As we were finishing, we spotted a dead, bloated cat floating in the cesspool in the basement area. Chris, the joker in the bunch, said, "We need to poke that cat with a stick." I firmly stated, "No way, I am not doing that." We thought it would be interesting but didn't want to smell the result. "Jeff, I dare you to poke it," Chris said. We had already put our gas masks away, and I didn't want to let the cat out of the bag. Pun intended. Suddenly, Chris grabbed a stick and poked the cat before we could say or do anything. Sure enough, it made a loud hissing noise as it deflated. I left the area immediately as I didn't want to smell it. The other guys got the cat in a bag and threw it away.

Every high school in California must have functional smoke alarms. When the construction at Acalanes High School faced unexpected delays, classes began, and to compound the challenges, the smoke alarms were found to be non-functional. Guess who got to solve this problem? Another worker and I became the human smoke alarms for six weeks, walking around the school halls looking for smoke.

I created my flashcards to assist with my learning and rote memorization in graduate school. This was particularly important in marine biology where there were countless definitions to regurgitate. I could develop figures and images on these flashcards to help my learning. Not only was filling out the flashcards helpful, but reviewing them was also valuable. Memorizing for me was agonizingly slow, and I would take a pile of flashcards with me wherever I went. Fortunately, I could review my flashcards while performing as a human smoke alarm.

What did I get from this work experience? First, I developed the ability to work with individuals from diverse backgrounds. Nobody is made the same, and I learned it takes practice to work with and understand people. Second, I learned, in a very clear way, that I was always going to have a boss and always going to have to follow directions. Third, working with these men who served their country helped me understand life outside my little bubble in Lafayette. They were adamant I needed to stay in school and make them proud. They didn't want to see me working there for the rest of my life. Ultimately, working for the school district strengthened my resilience for future challenges and served as a stepping stone to progressively better opportunities. It instilled in me a profound appreciation for all subsequent roles in my career.

Chapter Ten

Sacramento-San Joaquin Delta

It was March of 1992, and I had just finished my graduate school coursework, so I began my job search. I aimed to work with fish but didn't know where to start. Because this was before the wide use of the internet, I resorted to the environmental section of the Yellow Pages and started calling companies. For those of you who don't know, the Yellow Pages are telephone directories of businesses organized by category rather than alphabetically by business name. Households received an annually updated phone book with yellow pages. My phone call mostly went like this: "Hello, I am pursuing a graduate degree in marine biology, and I was wondering if you hire marine biologists?" They typically said, "We are an environmental company that does environmental testing. Sorry, we do not hire marine biologists." Most companies I talked with were soil testing companies. Then, I spoke with a fisheries consultant in Walnut Creek, California. After my excellent opening statement and question, the person said, "We hire fish biologists, but they must have experience." This was a start! I then asked if they knew of anyone hiring. They suggested contacting the local California Department of Fish and Game office. I was very appreciative of the help. I didn't know this then, but in the future I would be dueling with this consultant in front of the State Water Resources Control Board during water quality hearings.

I contacted the closest office, completed an application for a scientific aide position, and mailed it to them. A supervisor contacted me several weeks later and invited me to interview. I needed clarification during my interview, as the interviewer stated he worked for the U.S. Fish and Wildlife Service. Was I being interviewed for a job with the state or federal government?

I was hired as a biological science aide for six months in the Sacramento-San Joaquin Delta of California. The Delta is a large tidal area that mixes saltwater from the ocean with freshwater from the rivers that flow into it on the West Coast of the United States. It drains the Sacramento River and the San Joaquin River basins, and water from the Sierra Nevada and southern Cascade mountains also flows into it before reaching the ocean. The Delta comprises over 700 miles of sloughs and waterways.

The Delta was home to a rich abundance of fish and wildlife that used to have an immense amount of wetland habitat; however, the Delta was transformed in the 1800s by the construction of levees for flood control purposes. In the early 1900s, the Delta became one of the nation's largest water supply hubs. Upstream dams and reservoirs were constructed to capture valuable freshwater and control floods. Construction on the federal Central Valley Project began in 1937, and in 1960, California authorized the State Water Project.

The Central Valley Project and State Water Project were constructed to transfer water to Southern California. Since most of the rainfall in the state falls to the north, water must be conveyed to the drier south. The projects consist of upstream reservoirs that control water flow, levees to keep the water in rivers and the Delta and out of cities and agricultural lands, and a series of pumps, screens, and channels to move water.

Precipitation patterns in California are unpredictable, leading to droughts and floods. During dry periods, the state implements strict water conservation measures, while floods can put communities and businesses at risk during wet periods. The water conveyance system is crucial in managing floodwaters and providing water for agriculture, cities, and industries. Agriculture in the Central Valley, which benefited from fertile soils and water supply, thrived in the 18th century. Today, about 40% of

California's water runoff flows through the Delta, which supports about 25 million residents and six million acres of farmland.

As the Delta continued to get altered by humans historically, the habitat needed for native fish and wildlife changed. Water removal and channelization measures, including the construction of levees, agriculture, pollution, and development encroachment, are just some of the impacts on habitat. Approximately fifty-five types of fish and more than 750 wildlife species call the Delta home. Important native fish species with past commercial and recreational fishing value include salmon, steelhead, sturgeon, shad, anchovy, and herring. In addition, the Delta has become home to numerous invasive, non-native fish species, including striped and largemouth bass. Native fish are struggling even more due to recent impacts such as climate change. As of this book's writing, five species of fish are listed by the federal Endangered Species Act, including winter-run Chinook salmon, spring-run Chinook salmon, Central Valley steelhead, North American green sturgeon, and Delta smelt. All of these species were listed while I was working as a fish biologist.

In response to the water conveyance system and the need to monitor and study the fish populations of the Delta, a consortium of federal and state agencies formed a cooperative interagency studies program in the 1970s.

The Interagency Ecological Program consists of three California state agencies and six federal agencies with a stake in the Delta. Each agency plays a vital role in the Delta. The Department of Water Resources is the California agency that manages the state's water supply. The Department of Fish and Wildlife is the state agency that oversees the state's fish and wildlife, and the State Water Resources Control Board covers water rights, regulations, and laws surrounding water in California. The U.S. Bureau of Reclamation is the federal agency that manages the water supply. The U.S. Fish and Wildlife Service manages fish and wildlife. The U.S. Geological Survey is a federal agency that studies the country's natural resources. The U.S. Army Corps of Engineers is responsible for engineering and safety services associated with the nation. The National Marine Fisheries Service manages fish species of commercial value. Finally, the U.S. Environmental Protection Agency protects Americans from environmental health risks and enforces environmental regulations. Each of these agencies plays an important role. I share their jurisdictional responsibilities in the Delta to demonstrate the complexity of the fisheries biology career in the Central Valley of California. There is an immense need for fish biologists, ecologists, engineers, and statisticians in the various agencies of the Delta.

If this sounds confusing, that is because it is. Policy and science experts determined that the Delta is a "wicked" system with no solutions. Intense competing demands and complexity make management extremely difficult. Dyslexic individuals possess exceptional abilities to understand and work within complex systems. This appeared to be a good opportunity that would use my strengths.

Chapter Eleven

Juggling Work and School

I still remember my first day of work, which was terrific. I was on a boat that towed a net behind it, known as a trawl. The California Department of Fish and Game owned and operated the boat, and my new supervisor wore a U.S. Fish and Wildlife Service uniform. See why I was confused? We performed a series of tows with the net, bringing in a variety of fish. I was introduced to the local fish fauna and was trained to identify them. It was easy and fun, and I couldn't believe I was getting paid to do it. I was accustomed to working with fish due to my hobby of aquarium fish, and I quickly grasped fish identification and equipment operation.

My job entailed a lot of time trawling on boats, pulling a net through the water, and recording the results. I was also responsible for capturing fish at nearshore locations in the local waterways with a seine net. Work was to be done in the lab and the office when not trawling or seining. The lab work mainly consisted of removing and reading a small wire in the heads of juvenile salmon recovered in sampling, called a coded-wire-tag. These little tags are used to code unique groups of salmon and steelhead released at hatcheries to track survival in freshwater and the ocean. Salmon and steelhead that had tags in their heads would have a clipped fin, indicating that the fish had a tag in its head. Barely visible to the naked eye (about 1 mm long), the tags would contain a series of notches that translate into numeric codes. The fish head would be cut open under a dissecting scope to look for the tag. Once removed, the tag must be mounted on a holder and read with a microscope. When done, it would be put in a small bag and recorded on a data sheet. The little salmon would not survive this procedure. Coded-wire-tags are still used today; however, they have been supplemented with more advanced tagging procedures that can get more specific information, such as migration rate and route selection of fish. All the data collected in the field and the lab must be entered into databases so scientists and managers can use it.

I soon learned that I had worked for the U.S. Fish and Wildlife Service and had been ordered a uniform. There were approximately one dozen staff when I started working for the office. The long drives to sample sites and hours in the lab afforded many conversations, and I learned many had been in these temporary positions for a very long time. It was part of the field of fish biology. You had to learn to survive on lower salaries, potentially for years. I put on my persistence hat and hung on tight. I had learned to be persistent my entire life, as things didn't come quickly for me. This was no different.

It was exciting to start working in fisheries biology, yet I still needed to complete my master's degree. I did not want to be added to the list of people who stopped their graduate work before finishing. I still struggled with self-doubt, as I had a long road ahead of me to get my master's thesis completed, and I felt as if I was barely getting by in terms of grades. Another problematic class and a C, and I would have to reconsider finishing seriously. I worked with my advisor to choose a unique lab project for my thesis at San Francisco State. Most master's thesis students would find an ongoing project with their advisor and use that project for the thesis in some way. I decided to generate my data in the lab with a unique experimental design. My proficiency in strategic thinking played a crucial role in bringing about this outcome.

It was 1992, and I could not afford the cost of housing on a salary of $6.77 per hour. I qualified for poverty rates on utilities, but the rent was the same for all. I was told there would be more positions coming at higher salaries, just above poverty, and I did what I had to do to survive—I camped out of the back of my truck. After work, I would head to the gym and shower if available. Then, I would head to one of two campgrounds nearby. I would spend my evenings on the levee either fishing or just enjoying the view, and I would cook my food with a little camp stove. Fortunately, I could go to my parents' house in the East Bay over the weekends.

A typical day in the field would start at 6:00 a.m. at the office. The field crew would meet and collect the blank data sheets, sampling equipment, and miscellaneous supplies. The crew would then head to the sampling location in a government vehicle. This would be between one hour and two hours away in most cases. As the day unfolded, fish catches and environmental data were recorded on data sheets. Captures of fish varied considerably depending on the time of year and other factors. Sometimes, no fish would be captured, and the following site would be visited. In other cases, thousands of fish would be captured, causing long delays in identifying and measuring all the fish. When all the samples had been taken, it was time to return to the office.

At the office, field sheets would be reviewed for accuracy, equipment would be returned and charged as needed, and the following day's sampling would be prepared. Assuming no problems were experienced with boats, vehicles, or other delays, the day would be approximately eight hours long. Each field crew member would work about four days a week in the field, and the one remaining day would be spent in the lab or office entering data. Skills needed for this work included fish identification knowledge, measurement accuracy, and the ability to adjust in inclement weather and other unforeseen circumstances. Once, a sea lion got in our net, and we had to cut it out before the net came on board. Otherwise, a sea lion would have been chasing us on the boat! It was not uncommon to tow stranded boats to shore and to help the public on the Delta.

Doing this work was truly enjoyable. We had to work in diverse weather conditions, adapting to extreme cold, scorching heat, and wet environments. When catches reached unprecedented levels, we would be behind with our sample processing, and our days would be very long. Depending on the season, there were instances of retaining particular fish species for various purposes, whether clipping fins for future genetic analysis or bagging the entire fish for lab processing. Mastering the art of processing fish in challenging weather conditions with numb hands became a skill acquired through practice.

Occasionally, wind conditions would make collecting samples in the Western Delta difficult. Work would have to be halted if the boat couldn't maintain its position due to high winds or if crew members experienced seasickness. Sometimes, strong winds from the west would blow eastward, which, when combined with an outgoing tide, would create large waves. Generally, the boat would have a gentle roll, but the combination of a gentle roll and diesel fumes could cause some people to become seasick. However, I found that I could cope with bouts of seasickness better than most.

In October 1992, I accepted a temporary GS-5 Biological Science Technician position. While this position was temporary, the additional salary afforded me enough to live in a low-cost, one-bedroom apartment. Then, in January 1993, I was hired as a GS-7 Supervisory Fishery Biologist in a one-year position. When that position expired, I applied for and was hired into a second temporary position. I was one of two crew leads responsible for designing and leading monitoring efforts, scheduling the sampling, training, equipment procurement, data entry, quality control, analysis, and miscellaneous writing. I was gaining a lot of experience in fish biology, which I welcomed.

The exact schedule was followed every week throughout the year, and sometimes, scheduling was done seven days per week, which required working on weekends. I could earn overtime pay or compensatory time if I worked more than forty hours a week. Although the early start times and harsh weather conditions exhausted me, the pleasure of being outside and sampling fish helped me endure the tiredness.

I would use my annual leave and vacation days at the U.S. Fish and Wildlife Service to travel to San Francisco

State, where I worked with my advisor to develop my master's thesis plan. I set up 15 aquariums in the lab, each with one fish. I trained the fish to identify and consume prey by designing feeding plates crafted from plexiglass adorned with plastic aquarium plants. I was to test the hypothesis that fish would improve their search efficiency over time. To do this, I would have to check out video cameras from the video department to record the fish and then review the times in the videos on my video cassette recorder at home. It would have been wonderfully convenient if I had an iPhone, but this was the 1990s! I needed to do the filming during my vacations, as I was working full-time. I commuted from Lafayette to San Francisco with video equipment in tow during my vacations.

While education was a struggle for me, many U.S. Fish and Wildlife Service staff members only had bachelor's degrees in biology and were not necessarily fishheads like me. Some staff members were simply locals with enough college credits to qualify for entry-level positions. This began to change as the office started increasing in size and hiring more staff as we advertised job vacancies nationwide. Because I was an actual fish head, I began to acquire tasks of a fish biology nature, including proto-col writing, data summarization, graphing, and database programming, among other things.

I knew a colleague who was a friendly and easy-to-work-with Christian. However, he often made judgmental and caustic comments, which turned off many staff. Consequently, he quickly alienated himself and was eventually let go. As a Christian working in a secular government agency, I am protected from religious discrimination. Nevertheless, discussing religion at work can be tricky. My former colleague's experience taught me that discussing religion at work can have negative consequences.

I had been in four positions of a temporary nature when the U.S. Fish and Wildlife Service was ready to add permanent staff to the office. They advertised the permanent positions, and I applied with zeal. To get a job, I had to fill out an application, answer a series of essay questions called Knowledge, Skills, and Abilities, otherwise known as KSAs, and submit a resume with transcripts showing specific coursework and degrees. Fortunately, there were no multiple-choice questions, and this task was easy for me as I had plenty of context to answer the questions. A list would be produced, ranking all applicants if they qualified. There was a maximum of one hundred points possible, and you needed to be among the top-ranked candidates to be hired. This typically meant you'd need a score of at least ninety-five. Applicants could apply as often as necessary, and I applied several times until my score was in the upper nineties.

I was selected for a permanent GS-9 Supervisory Fish Biologist position, Field Crew Leader, in February 1995, three years after starting my first position. I was required to do more fish biology tasks, including analysis and writing, as well as the everyday supervisor tasks, such as hiring, evaluating, and training staff. This involved a host of new duties I needed to familiarize myself with. I developed the work schedule, sampling protocols, training programs, and responsibilities of up to fifteen employees. However, the primary focus of my job was to determine how many salmon and steelhead were moving through the Delta and where they moved and resided in the different channels. The results of this information were seasonally dependent and were used to inform water operations and future reports, permits, and peer-reviewed literature. I learned how to develop database programs to summarize salmon and juvenile fish catch statistics automatically. I frequently provided catch information to my boss and on inter-agency conference calls and meetings.

Working full-time and trying to complete my master's thesis was not easy. I was mentally and sometimes physically exhausted at the end of the day, and it took considerable motivation to work after hours on my thesis. I was beginning to see the finish line but was still concerned about my grades.

I was in a rapid monitoring experimentation phase that lasted several years at work. This was a good fit for me, as people with dyslexia are particularly adept at generating creative solutions in a problem-solving context. Scientific studies show significant increases in creativity between dyslexic and nondyslexic adults. This was my world; my brain was constructed to develop ideas to address problems. I would wake up many mornings with my mind brimming with excitement and fresh ideas. I couldn't wait to get to work and share my thoughts.

I am grateful to have been allowed to try new things. We attempted numerous new gear types, some of which failed. For example, we tried push netting with a net in front of the boat. The end of the net would be beneath the boat but not far enough to get stuck in the propeller. A large frame held a net in front of the boat, pushing it through the water. Ultimately, push netting needed to be better at catching fish, as the net was small and difficult to tow fast enough. We began rotary screw trapping at new locations at this time. A rotary screw trap is a cone-shaped trap suspended between two floating pontoons. It spins in the water, trapping fish in the process. We purchased the traps, constructed them at boat ramps, and towed them to the sample sites. Affixing them to trees or other permanent structures on the banks of the river, we would check the traps most days for salmon catches. For years, our endeavors proved highly effective in capturing juvenile salmon of all sizes, establishing rotary screw traps as the preferred sampling gear, a status they maintain to this day. One problem with screw traps is that they must be secured when high outflow events occur, or they can get destroyed. One New Year's Eve, I had to tow a trap off the river late at night during a storm. That was a memorable way to spend New Year's Eve.

Individuals with dyslexia excel at learning from experience, and I was at home. Trying new techniques, adjusting, and persevering through complex fisheries sampling methods delighted me. I could not believe I was getting paid to play in the local rivers so that I could catch more fish. We were getting more efficient at setting up rotary screw traps. Some sites didn't have an excellent tree to tie up these traps. One year, I searched for a giant anchor to set the trap in the middle of the Sacramento River. I found an 88-pound Danforth anchor. We secured it to a long chain and towed the rotary screw trap to the middle of the river, and tossed the anchor overboard. The anchor dug into the substrate immediately, and the trap was held in the middle of the river. When we returned at the end of the season to remove the trap and anchor, we discovered we could not get the anchor up. It had been buried too deep. So, there is an 88-pound anchor on the bottom of the Sacramento River. Sorry!

In addition, we continued to look for more suitable trawling operations and began experiments with a Kodiak net.

This trawl operation, developed in Kodiak, Alaska, uses two boats to pull a sizeable top-oriented net. This net proved to be more effective at capturing juvenile fish, and it continues to be used today.

The boss needed a way to estimate the number of fish captured in trawling and seining operations understandable to politicians, the media, engineers, and all stakeholders involved in the fish world. I was ecstatic when he pulled me from the field to work on this task. I developed the Sacramento Catch Index to estimate the movement of juvenile winter-run Chinook salmon. This was a novel trigger system used to cause specific management actions. If fish catch reaches a trigger level, they cause a management action such as closing gates to prevent water and fish from going in the wrong direction. The trigger system I developed over twenty years ago continues to be used today, unchanged. My creativity and innovation were a part of this catch-index development.

I continued working for the Interagency Ecological Program. I enjoyed working with colleagues at other agencies, such as the California Department of Fish and Game and the U.S. National Marine Fisheries Service. We shared staff, equipment, and office space. We also had annual meetings at Asilomar, a resort-style conference center along the coast of California. We ate meals together and had after-hours parties every night. These meetings were a tradition for many years until visiting nice destinations for annual meetings became inappropriate. Letting off steam together and getting to know each other at a conference was critical to the program's success. Unfortunately, it is no longer permitted, but I understand how the public could perceive it poorly.

We used to have our lunch in the large break room at the office. Generally, the senior staff members would sit on one side of the room while the rest of us sat on the other side. As I moved up the ladder in the organization, I started having my lunch with the senior staff, and I got to know the executive staff of both the California Department of Fish and Game (now known as the California Department of Fish and Wildlife) and the U.S. Fish and Wildlife Service. Eventually, I was requested to lead multi-agency work teams.

The state executive with the nice corner office of the building was a friendly, Christian man, and I noticed he had a large aquarium in his office when I was walking by one day. I poked my head in and looked at the messy aquarium. It housed a large oscar, a popular tropical aquarium fish. I had kept many oscars in the past. He looked at me and said, "I don't know what to do with that fish. The tank is a mess, and the fish keeps getting larger." I told him it needed some care and offered to clean the tank. He happily accepted, and I now cared for the big boss's fish. He was almost always gone at meetings, and I would clean the aquarium for him when he was out.

I had finished all my master's thesis work, including the filming and associated analysis. Fortunately, my employer was gracious enough to let me use my work computer, including statistical programs, to finish my thesis. I could use the computer at work after hours to produce drafts of the thesis document, run statistical tests, and start working on slides for my thesis defense.

Most of my thesis writing was finally completed, and I was approaching the seven-year limit. If one takes longer than seven years, they must take more classes, which was not appealing. It had taken me a long time to get to the end—so long that one of the professors on my committee had retired.

I discovered evidence of search image formation, as my thesis fish improved their foraging rates with experience. In 1996, I drove to Carmel Valley to have my master's thesis signed off by the retired professor and then took it to the Biology Department at San Francisco State University. The rest of my committee signed it. I defended my thesis soon after that and was done one year ahead of the seven-year limit. I remember my parents came to my thesis defense, and we went to a fancy seafood place in San Francisco afterward. My parents, heroes who fought for me for decades, celebrated this accomplishment with me. For an exciting read, check out *Improvement of Foraging in Cichlasoma nigrofasciatum: Search Image or Search*

Rate? by Jeffrey McLain, 1996, San Francisco State University.

Before I close the book on my San Francisco State degree, I must share something else. I was on academic probation at San Francisco State for nearly the entire time. You must maintain a grade point average (GPA) of 3.0 to graduate, and I was hovering around the 2.8 zone for almost two years. When I applied for graduation, I had a GPA of 2.95, and I was denied. Fortunately, my master's thesis research class grade was yet to be issued. It was an A, and my GPA was at 3.02. By the skin of my teeth, I graduated.

In 1997, I was promoted to a higher level at the U.S. Fish and Wildlife Service. I was moved to staff supervisor and lead fishery biologist for the long-term monitoring and special study projects focusing on salmon and steelhead. This was a GS-11 position that supervised professional fishery biologists and wage grade small craft operators. This position involved more office leadership and human resource skills than prior positions and increased my report writing and publication duties. Of course, all these activities are something you learn by doing or learn by taking agency-specific training.

I was excited to work on my first publication with a colleague. We produced a seminal publication titled *Juvenile Chinook salmon abundance, distribution, and survival in the Sacramento-San Joaquin Estuary.*[1] This document summarized over twenty years of salmon monitoring and survival data and became a popular and helpful document in salmon biology. During this time, I started several other publications, which took me a number of years to complete.

I was encouraged to publish the results of a salmon study I implemented in the North Delta by Randy Brown, an executive who worked for the Department of Water Resources. He was convinced that the work I had done thus far on juvenile salmon was vital. Randy was a mentor of mine and always encouraging. I completed fieldwork in the early 2000s, and it took considerable time to get my manuscript through reviews in the San Francisco Estuary Watershed Science journal. During the midst of my peer-review work, tragedy struck as Randy passed away suddenly due to a heart attack.

Eventually, I published a paper on nearshore salmon use in the North Delta, titled *Nearshore areas used by fry Chinook salmon, <u>Oncorhynchus tshawytscha</u>, in the Northwest-*

---

1. Brandes, P.L. and McLain, J.S. 2001. Juvenile Chinook salmon abundance, distribution, and survival in the Sacramento-San Joaquin Estuary. Fish Bulletin 179 (2).

ern Sacramento-San Joaquin Delta, California.[2] I carried this document through several positions and agencies to get it over the finish line. This manuscript took longer than anticipated, but I stuck with it. Persistence is one of my strong suits.

In my role as a supervisor, I encountered challenging issues that no amount of formal education had equipped me to handle. You don't know their full backgrounds when you work with and supervise others. You only know what they tell you. You also can't predict how they will react in certain situations or how factors outside work will impact them. For example, smoking is prohibited on federal watercraft. What would you do if someone was a chain smoker and couldn't work on a boat without a cigarette for more than an hour or two? Would you allow them to break the rule and permit them to smoke on the boat? Or would you let the entire crew drive the boat back to the dock, frequently allowing smoke breaks? What if the employee was a good worker and attended smoking cessation courses? What if they fought for their country and were a decorated veteran? The answer to these types of situations is never easy. I don't know why the person started smoking, and since I wasn't a smoker, I didn't

---

2. McLain, J., and G. Castillo. 2009. Nearshore areas used by fry Chinook salmon, *Oncorhynchus tshawytscha*, in the Northwestern Sacramento-San Joaquin Delta, California. San Francisco Estuary & Watershed Science, 7(2).

understand nicotine addiction. I treated this situation with a lot of empathy and listening. I recall offering smoking cessation classes, and the employee tried nicotine patches and various means to stop or at least reduce the smoking. Ultimately, the employee understood they could not meet the job requirements due to the addiction and failure to control it. Did I let this employee go too long? Others likely think I did. This example serves as a good one for many human resource issues a manager must resolve. There is often no correct answer, and eventually, policies must be followed.

Other situations were more clear-cut. I had one employee behaving oddly—repeatedly running out of gas in a government vehicle, working extremely hard for days, and then missing several work days. This employee's coworkers knew much more about what was happening than I did. Eventually, an employee reported some serious safety matters to me, and after investigation, I found them to be true. This was my first termination, and it felt terrible.

My supervisor then suggested I read after hours to improve my writing abilities. He suggested classic literature by authors such as Henry David Thoreau and Edgar Allan Poe. I embarked on this task for several years and did find it helpful. Some of this reading was difficult for me; however, I believe it continued to help my dyslexic brain adjust. At that time, I discovered John Steinbeck, who became one of my favorite authors.

Marty was the head of the office and was a good mentor and leader. I learned he was a Christian. He was a calm, well-respected fish biologist with a doctorate in fisheries sciences. I also knew that many of the executives from other agencies had a Christian faith, although it was not something they openly shared in the workplace. Marty would invite the entire office to his home every Christmas. This became a huge burden as the size of the crew was growing. His wife passed away from a tough battle with cancer, leaving him a widow before retiring. I went to her memorial service and found her a pillar in their church, having started numerous Bible studies and programs. I grasped that Marty, along with several others in upper management, held profound religious beliefs, and the influence of his wife was also noteworthy. However, I was still not convinced I should mix religion with work.

I often tell people that government employees need high emotional intelligence (EQ). It is not a job for everyone. The benefits of high EQ include understanding your emotions, learning from your mistakes, reasonable control of your impulses and thoughts, and empathy skills. I was becoming aware that my dyslexia afforded me many of these skills. Like my test-taking difficulties, I couldn't put my finger on it at the time, but over time it became evident.

Chapter Twelve

A Huge Aquarium

I was making a decent salary and had a permanent job, and it was time to make a serious aquarium commitment. I contacted a company in Arizona and started building my dream aquarium over the phone with them. I needed something huge, but not so large that I would need a crane to move it. I also needed to clear this aquarium with my landlord, as I rented an apartment then. I decided on a custom 440-gallon plexiglass tank with an integrated filtration system. This aquarium was unique because it had a lifetime guarantee against leakage.

It took several months for them to build the aquarium, and the anticipation was incredible. I remember the day it got delivered, like it was yesterday. They kept asking me if I would have a moving crew to receive the tank because they said they would not move the aquarium into my apartment. They needed more people to move it. That should have been a warning, but it didn't register. They said it would be delivered sometime that week but couldn't tell me the time.

Sure enough, I was told they would be at my apartment shortly. I ran home from work to find the truck in the parking lot of my apartment complex. The driver was in the back of the truck, and there was my aquarium. It was so heavy it crushed the pallet. The aquarium was eight feet long, three feet high, and two feet deep. It weighed 660 pounds empty and came complete with the stand and a canopy over the top. The delivery man asked, "Where is your crew?" I immediately got on the phone and called my moving crew, who were all at work. He got the aquarium from the truck with a palette jack and hydraulic lift. It sat in the parking lot until my crew came later that afternoon. I moved the aquarium into the apartment with eight large guys—three on each end and one in the middle of the aquarium on each side. It was huge for an apartment. I needed a ladder to get into it and clean it. The best way to clean it was to empty half the water, climb inside the tank, walk around, and wipe the walls. The fish didn't like that, but tough. They should have been grateful to have such luxury!

Equipped with a massive aquarium, I eagerly anticipated filling it with sizable fish. Yet, a challenge emerged—the scarcity of local aquarium stores offering large fish of this kind. Eventually, I found an inspiring aquarium store approximately one hour away called Capitol Aquarium. This was a gigantic aquarium store with many tanks filled with fish of all sizes. In the back of the store, they would keep large fish in bathtub-sized tanks. This was a fish lover's paradise. I acquired some of my favorite fresh-water tropical fish. First was peacock bass. These are predatory cichlids that get close to three feet long. They are famous for fighting at the end of a fishing line, and people fly from all parts of the globe to fish for them in their native habitat in South America. They are extremely fast and would dart across the tank and gobble up live fish food at amazing speed. I also acquired a large pacu. These are large, deep-bodied fish that are gentle giants. I used to feed this one hot dogs and potatoes from my hand. It grew quickly in my aquarium, reaching several feet in length. I remember purchasing a giant emperor catfish. The following day, I noticed one of my favorite fish was missing, and there was a lump in the emperor catfish's belly. That catfish was returned!

I would get frequent visitors. People would be walking by the apartment and suddenly stop and stare through the window. I would invite them in and explain the fish and the tank. Kids would refuse to leave. I had that aquarium for numerous years, moved it to my first house, and, unfortunately, used the same poor moving crew. We broke the ramp to the rental truck while moving the tank. It was fun explaining to the moving company how I broke the ramp. I couldn't find a suitable spot to keep the aquarium in my new home. I was hoping I could use the aquarium as a tool to minister to kids by donating it to the 180 Teen Center, a local youth center in Lodi. Kids were interested in video games and other things, not aquariums. Second, the aquarium was in an area without air conditioning and got too warm. I would dump bags of ice in it every few days to keep the temperature down. I couldn't find anyone to help me maintain the aquarium, so we sold it and donated the money to the youth center.

Chapter Thirteen

Europe

In June 1999, my family and I went on a three-week trip to Europe, which was a dream come true for us. We traveled to Scotland, Ireland, Wales, and finally, London. We rented a car during the trip and stayed at bed-and-breakfasts and hotels. Our main objective was to visit Duart Castle, located on the Isle of Mull in Scotland, which is the ancestral home of the McLain clan. The castle was built in the 14th century as a residence for the Highland Maclean clan and has undergone restoration work since 1911. It is worth noting that 'McLain' can be spelled in many different ways, and it is possible to trace which part of the family you come from based on the spelling. The castle has a dungeon, which made us realize that the McLains meant serious business!

We also visited many churches throughout our trip, and I was surprised by how these tours impacted me. Our first visit was to St. Giles' Cathedral in Edinburgh, a gigantic and beautiful cathedral founded in the 12th century. My journal says, "It's been a long time since I felt that inner peace and happiness." Several days later, we visited St. John's Episcopal Church in Edinburgh, which has the best stained-glass collection in Scotland.

We then headed to Ireland, visiting Christ Church Cathedral in Dublin and Trinity College to see the Book of Kells. We had several days in London before departing, and we visited Westminster Abbey, which left me speechless. The rest of the family then headed in a different direction to a museum, and I headed to St. Paul's Cathedral. I toured the cathedral thoroughly with a purchased guidebook in hand. I was amazed at the history and basked in the warmth and presence of centuries of prayer and parishioners. I felt the presence of God in the churches I visited—they were living, working symbols of the Christian faith. A draw to these churches, comfort, peace, and warmth, was something I had never experienced before. The booklet purchased at Westminster Abbey welcomes the visitor with a beautiful statement:

"Whatever the reason for your visit, we hope that you will encounter the presence of God, to whom this place of prayer is dedicated, and sense the long history of this house of kings."

Though the buildings were empty of parishioners, I still felt God's presence. God continues to speak through empty churches, and I am thankful for that.

Upon returning from our trip, I immediately purchased a copy of the Holy Bible and read it avidly from cover to cover. I was searching for something, and while the books about evolution remained untouched on the shelf, I knew I had found what I was looking for.

Chapter Fourteen

A Purpose

Several months later, I visited family in Lafayette, California, for Thanksgiving break. My sister and I decided on an invigorating and lengthy hike with friends. My sister's friend brought a beautiful young lady along, and we talked continuously during the hike. It was as if only two of us were hiking alone. I'd always enjoyed my sister's friends, but I never thought I would be introduced to my future spouse through those friends.

I had never met anyone as lovely as Anne before. We had many things in common. We grew up swimming competitively, we went to the same high school (I am five years older, so we didn't know each other), and she was a teacher at the school where my mom taught. They knew each other before we knew each other. I returned to work after that break and continuously had Anne on my mind. Shortly after that, I ran into her again while visiting my mom at school, and we arranged for another hike. This time, I learned she was a committed Christian and had faithfully attended church all her life. I also discovered we were both reading the Bible and in the book of Judges. The Bible contains more than 1,200 pages of text and sixty-six books. The book of Judges recounts the history of Israel, how the people rebelled, and how God brought judgment upon them. It is a foundational book that reminds the reader they are sinful. We were both studying this book simultaneously and struggling through similar questions. This seemed like serendipity to me, and I wondered if this was fate somehow.

Anne's family has a coveted cookie recipe, and she baked cookies frequently. I would come to understand it was relaxing for her. This worked perfectly because I found it comforting to eat them! Not just the family chocolate chip oatmeal cookie but peanut butter cookies, snickerdoodles, and many other types. She quickly realized I enjoyed the cookies because I jumped up and down like a little kid when she brought them to me! It seemed like I had stumbled upon a treasure.

It wasn't long before we dated exclusively, even though we were several hours apart. We talked frequently on the phone during the week, and I would stay at my parents' house on weekends to spend time together. She was very encouraging, as she knew I was seeking answers and spending a lot of time reading the Bible. She also encouraged me to visit churches, and I started doing that. It was as if Anne came along at just the right time in my life when I was seeking answers.

Armed with degrees in the sciences, including courses in paleontology and functional morphology of animals, I believed I had a reasonably firm grasp on how things came to be. I didn't get my degrees from a private Christian college but from two public universities. I don't recall learning anything about Christianity or faith in college. One memory that sticks with me is that my world history professor clarified that he was not religious. After a long rant about religion, he summed up his thoughts by saying, "Religion is nothing but a money-making enterprise." That sums up what I learned about Christianity in college!

Nevertheless, the evolution of entire groups of organisms (taxa) was a stretch for me. It felt like the topic of evolution and Christianity were mutually exclusive and that I needed to resolve this issue in my head. Evolution supposedly happens gradually over time, causing new taxa to be formed. Yet there is a shockingly deplete amount of evidence of gradual changes over time. Mostly, what is seen is taxa just appearing in the fossil record. Some organisms stuck, and some disappeared. Supporters of evolutionary theory claim the evidence will be found eventually, yet there are so many gaps and still no evidence of gradual transitions between taxa.

One example that bothered me involved fish. My favorite group of fishes, called cichlids (remember, a few chapters back?), actually have two jaws. They have an oral jaw, which we see—the mouth. They also have a pharyngeal jaw, a grinding mechanism with teeth in the upper mouth. This amazing fact allows cichlids to capture prey with their oral jaws and to further process their prey quickly with the pharyngeal jaw. This is why cichlids are such messy aquarium fish. They masticate their food, releasing little bits of food and bones. But I am digressing. These special jaws are believed to have evolved twice separately and can be found in several other groups of fish. Scientists still don't have evidence of how this extra jaw evolved. The belief is it evolved from the gill rakers, yet there is no evidence. No intermediate forms. Nothing. I share this simple example of something staring me in the face. If we can't find evidence of the gradual evolution of a part of a fish's mouth, how can we find evidence of entire organisms and taxa evolving into others?

I am a scientist, trained to believe we have all the answers. As we get more answers, we discover more we don't know. Like a true scientist, I began reading Christian apologetics books to investigate the Bible and Christianity. Unlike evolutionary theory, which attempts to explain how things worked in the past, the Christian faith is firmly rooted in history, with significant evidence backing up the claims.

For me, this all started with the Bible. I learned of its origins and historical accuracy. The Bible is a collection of texts inspired by God and recorded on various surfaces, such as stone and parchment. Before the development of the printing press, the Bible was communicated orally among people. Eventually, oral traditions were put into manuscripts centuries before the birth of Christ. Scribes followed strict standards, ensuring accuracy, and a lot of information exists documenting their methods. How do we know this? One way is the Dead Sea Scrolls, which are dated to a time before the birth of Christ. The Dead Sea Scrolls show no change whatsoever in the Bible since before the birth of Christ and are identical to specific sections of the Old Testament Bible we read today. Before the printing press, scribes copied the Bible letter by letter, taking more than a year to complete. The historical accuracy of the Bible is striking, and it explains why it is one of the most dependable historical documents in existence. Modern archaeology has found thousands of verified biblical facts that can be related and verified to nearly every book of the Bible.

The evidence that Jesus Christ was crucified and rose three days after is also true. The number of witnesses to Jesus' resurrection exceeded 500 people. Famous lawyers and judges applied the rules of evidence to the resurrection accounts, finding them valid. Backing up the resurrection of Jesus Christ is the fact that his disciples continued to profess that he was resurrected and the savior for decades beyond his crucifixion.

There are two types of faith: emotional and intellectual. Emotional faith is not based on facts but on feelings. One may believe in Jesus Christ since childhood. Or it may be one feels the presence of God, creating an emotional faith. An intellectual faith is based on facts—the biblical record, archaeological record, resurrection, etc. I believe most people have a mixture of these two types of faith; however, some may have an overwhelming amount of one or the other. I think I entered Christianity primarily with intellectual faith and experienced emotional faith after.

It is thought that there are relatively few Christian scientists; however, I am not the first. Many scientists, far more intelligent and famous than me, are believers. For example, Gregor Mendel, the father of genetics, was an abbot for the Catholic church. Francis Collins, a famous physician and geneticist who led the discovery of the DNA gene map, among other things, became convinced there is a God and designer. He wrote a best seller called *The Language of God: A Scientist Presents Evidence for Belief.* In a more recent example, Dr. Kizzmekia Corbett, who led the team of scientists that developed the Moderna vaccine against COVID-19, is a committed Christian.

I was convinced by the evidence behind the Holy Bible and committed my life to Jesus Christ. This helped me find happiness and contentment, knowing that my sins had been forgiven and that I was created and loved by God. My priorities changed as I became less focused on myself and more focused on others. I added prayer to my life, bringing my family and my stresses before God, significantly reducing my stress.

I believe you cannot accept Jesus into your heart and only believe the convenient parts of the gospel. I believe God created the universe and everything in it. I believe in the Word of God (the Bible), and the Word of God says God created the universe and all living matter. I believe in the Trinity, that there is a God as Father, a Son who is Jesus Christ, and the Holy Spirit, and they are one.

I became a life-long learner and student of the Bible. This didn't set me above others and make me a better person. It didn't guarantee my success or my happiness. It didn't ensure I wouldn't have a life filled with difficulty and struggles. It was not some secret cure or secret to my success, and it wouldn't guarantee my prosperity. It also doesn't mean I have all the answers, particularly to those difficult questions from studying the Bible. However, I weighed the evidence and found far more evidence in Christianity than evolution. I understand this is difficult for many to understand, particularly scientists.

I want to draw attention to the fact that I hold a particular belief regarding my dyslexia and my faith. While some may think I assert I was healed of my dyslexia by Jesus, I do not share that view. Instead, I believe that God allows things to happen for a reason. In this case, my dyslexia is a part of my unique journey and experience, and although it was challenging, it has shaped me into who I am today. While I am grateful for any help I receive, I also believe that everything happens for a purpose, even if it is not always immediately apparent to us.

I went through a struggle of faith and science and believe that God had me all along—and that He is the one who put my purpose in place. God knows our plans before we do, and His time is of a different scale than ours. I just didn't know it. I owe all I have to God for creating my passion for fish and my unique abilities. He made me, and He designed me for a purpose.

My purpose in life became apparent as I understood the internal struggle of evolution and my faith. I understood my potential and goal to serve God. How would I fulfill my purpose?

I walked into my boss Marty's office one morning and interrupted him to tell him I had given my life to Christ. He immediately jumped out of his chair and hugged me with tears in his eyes. Marty is approaching ninety years old as I write this book, and I enjoy lunch with him occasionally.

Chapter Fifteen

A Marriage

That Christmas of 1999, I met Anne's parents for the first time. We had a pleasant visit, and her mom was filled with questions about fish and my job. Her mom had such a fantastic way with people (the apple doesn't fall far from the tree.) I was driving Anne home that night, and I held her hand and felt God's provision. That is when I knew she was the one.

We were married in February 2001. Anne finished her teaching position in the East Bay and then moved to Lodi, California, my home for several years. We were actively looking for churches in our city. After having visited several churches, including one church, for more than six months, we stumbled into a North American Baptist church, and it didn't take long for us to understand it was our home. We immediately connected with many people at our age and stage in life. Anne was Presbyterian, I was

Episcopalian, and we were both baptized as infants. It was time for us to get baptized as adults, and we took the plunge on February 16, 2003.

My marriage to Anne filled many of our personality voids wonderfully. Anne has coached swimming for many years and is a professional elementary school teacher. She comes from a family of teachers; many of her friends are also teachers. She has skills in child behavior and teaching that I lack. Many other skills that I lack, such as remembering names and tracking details, are possessed by Anne. She is friendly, humble, and tactful in awkward situations. The benefits of marrying a teacher extend to the family and raising children. Anne is an excellent parent and has helped us raise two exceptional daughters. I contribute differently; Anne can't stand rodents and isn't particularly drawn to yard work or home repair, so I offer manual labor, emotional support, persistence, and hard work. We continuously help each other out. We troubleshoot problems with family, work, and friends together.

One day, Anne came home from work; she taught third grade at a local elementary school. She had a book called *Overcoming Dyslexia* by Sally Shaywitz, M.D. "The school district requires me to take training, and I thought this was a good topic," she explained. Of course, she was aware of my struggle growing up with dyslexia. I was intrigued, and I decided to read the book as well. My world was rocked.

The book provided the latest updates on dyslexia research. As I read in detail about dyslexia, the symptoms of the problem, and the actual upsides to the condition, my eyes were opened. There was a lot of familiar information—for example, one of the clues of dyslexia in early childhood is the difficulty learning nursery rhymes and a general lack of appreciation of such rhymes. My mind returned to my early childhood, feeling very different and odd, as I had trouble participating in nursery rhymes. I felt like an outcast. In another example, people with dyslexia are known to have difficulty remembering basic rote memory information. I struggled substantially with geography as a child, and I didn't learn the months of the year until high school. I never knew states' capitals; I still don't remember them. Anne and my children learned and can recall this rote memory information today. I was reminded of the trouble memorizing oaths and speeches in the Webelos, causing me to discontinue.

Reading about these signs and clues of dyslexia was very validating for me. I also learned about the gifts the dyslexia condition offered. Individuals with dyslexia can be excellent writers as long as the spelling is not necessary and the content is. They also make excellent science, medicine, architecture, law, policy, and finance experts. After reading *Overcoming Dyslexia,* I felt I had been given a gift. The decades-long difficulty in school began to fade. I started to realize I was held up against the standards of grades and tests in school, and because of my disability, I didn't appear to have much of a future. However, I learned that my disability likely led to a shift in brain function, prompting me to compensate and develop unique skills. These unusual skills made me particularly suitable for specific jobs and careers in the sciences. I found a promising career in my hobby that used my disability positively. I am thankful there was a plan for my future, and I thank God for this success.

Chapter Sixteen

Senior Fish Biologist

In 2001, I was promoted to habitat restoration coordinator for the U.S. Fish and Wildlife Service. Restoration coordinators play a pivotal role in restoring habitat for fish and wildlife. They work with agency partners to find willing landowners and funds to implement restoration projects. In my case, I focused on anadromous fish, such as salmon and steelhead, in the Central Valley of California.

The life of a restoration coordinator is an interesting one. For example, I coordinated several large restoration projects on the Tuolumne River. In this case, the restoration's overall intent was to improve the habitat for Chinook salmon. Over the years, human activities such as construction of dams, mining, and encroachment have caused damage to the river. As a result, the river needed to be restored by changing its shape, depth, and overall characteristics. I had to understand the dynamics of river processes and the specific aspects of those processes on the various life stages of the target fish (salmon). I needed to intimately understand the watershed's hydrograph to calibrate restoration projects for fish and flood conveyance properly. Additionally, I was responsible for acquiring funds through the federal and state grant systems, tracking costs during implementation, and managing all the environmental permits. I commonly carried a portfolio exceeding 30 million dollars of restoration projects.

The number of people and agencies I worked with and the breadth of knowledge to do the job was considerable. The advantages of a seasoned restoration coordinator are huge. They know how rivers work, what agency, and who in that agency to contact to get things done. After the project is built, post-project monitoring is needed to evaluate the conditions after construction, the survival of vegetation, and evaluation of the overall designs of the project.

Restoration work is a slow process that involves extensive planning, permits, proposals, and funding before any work can begin. Large projects also require public outreach and may involve litigation. A habitat restoration coordinator typically completes only a few projects in their career. This role may only be suitable for some, but someone like me, who is persistent and accustomed to slow processes, may find it well-suited.

The money behind the restoration projects was typically federal or state funds and considered public money. In addition, my salary and that of my colleagues were paid by government money. Because of this, accountability and tracking of resources related to restoration and our expenditures were taken extremely seriously to avoid a waste of public assets.

This job required much time on the road, driving to meetings and remote river locations. I recall driving several hours away to a field visit with a colleague. Shortly after leaving the office, we began an intense, hour-long conversation about Christianity, Jesus, and religious topics. I shared my testimony with him and stressed the need for Christ in his life. He needed to be more convinced but was respectful. I continue to have an excellent working relationship with this man.

As part of my job, I was responsible for promoting communication, encouraging teamwork, and sharing knowledge among different agencies and stakeholders to improve anadromous fish populations. To achieve this, I had to possess significant knowledge of restoration ecology and work closely with people. I usually met potential restoration partners at watershed meetings and stakeholder groups. Developing trust and relationships with potential partners was crucial before initiating restora-

tion projects. I enjoyed spending time with property own-
ers and potential restoration partners over meals and
tours. This job was an excellent fit for me.

Mining operations continue in many watersheds to this
day. Aggregate is needed for construction purposes, and
because a significant portion of the aggregate cost is
transport, local materials are required. I met someone
from a prominent aggregate company on the Merced
River at a stakeholder meeting and got to know them. I
asked to tour their plant conveniently close to the Merced
River. We started talking about a restoration project. The
aggregate companies had equipment that could move
levee material and spawning gravel around quickly. I set
up a project that benefitted us both. I convinced them to
shape the river since the aggregate company had equipment along the river. This resulted in tremendous cost
savings.

One of my jobs was representing the U.S. Fish and
Wildlife Service on the Tuolumne River Federal Energy
Regulatory Commission technical advisory committee. A
settlement was reached in 1995 that required instream
flows, habitat restoration, and other actions. I provided
instream flow and restoration advice, mainly at a series
of meetings. I was not happy with the paltry amount of
water let out of the dam for salmon, and other environmental organizations felt the same way. Unfortunately, it
was a settlement, and we had to live with it. I summarized

my thoughts on the settlement agreement in a peer-reviewed journal article titled *Managing the Tuolumne River for Salmonids: Assessment of the 1995 Settlement Agreement.*[1] This was my last peer-reviewed publication before entering the management world.

Writing peer-reviewed scientific articles is challenging for most; however, I found my writing was not hindered by dyslexia. Spell check on the computer helped, and I didn't seem to have trouble getting my thoughts into narrative format. This was mainly because I had been reading and writing so much that I was getting accustomed to it. I also had the advantage of knowing much of the background and context.

In 2004, I transferred to the National Marine Fisheries Service to broaden my experience. I remember my interview entailed a walk to Starbucks and a discussion with two staff members from the office. I had worked with both of these individuals for many years in my capacity at the U.S. Fish and Wildlife Service. This was the most casual job interview I have ever experienced. It involved a walk to a coffee shop where the two people explained the job and asked if I was interested. I said yes and received a generous offer and raise a few days later. I especially liked the Starbucks across the street from the office.

---

1. McLain, J. 2010. Managing the Tuolumne River for Salmonids: Assessment of the 1995 Settlement Agreement. California Fish and Game, 96(3): 173-187.

My oldest daughter was born in 2003, and we were expecting another daughter in 2005. There were better times to start a job in Sacramento, and we contemplated relocating to shorten my commute. We decided against moving, as we liked our current living situation in Lodi, which had become our home. Anne was job-sharing, and she could be home two days a week. The National Marine Fisheries Service offered telework, and I could pick up and drop off at childcare on other days. I could do this for several years before the kids went to school, and I am thankful for the flexibility.

The National Marine Fisheries Service has regulatory responsibilities for fish of commercial value, such as salmon, steelhead trout, and green sturgeon. They also manage coastal stocks of commercial value. They work with federal, state, and local partners to list species on the Endangered Species Act and recover and protect marine species. There are a few other laws and processes that the National Marine Fisheries Service uses, and as an employee, one must become familiar with these laws to do the job. I recall some people had these laws memorized, and they could cite them in conversation. The memorization of laws and policies is in the rote memory category and was a struggle for me. Fortunately, it was not a requirement for the job, and I could carry a copy of the laws and check them if needed.

As a senior-level fishery biologist, I wrote letters, reports, and documents about the impacts of activities affecting listed salmonids and sturgeon. This process is called Endangered Species Act consultation. I was also required to look at projects and initiatives from a high-level or big-picture perspective. Extra-large documents and processes were acceptable for me, as I was particularly good at finding the gist of the overall message as long as I could acquire context from the materials. Once I get my bearings, I look deeper into the topic, uncovering layers of meanings. I enjoyed working in an environment with deadlines and statutory requirements, which I found motivating.

Documents associated with large projects are often very long and must be looked at quickly. I remember once, I got called to meet at the loading dock for a copy of a document for a project. I thought it was a box. Nope, it was five boxes filling the back of a truck. While that example is extreme, receiving documents with thousands of pages of information was not uncommon. My dyslexic brain was designed for tasks such as these. While I had trouble deciphering abstract details in multiple-choice tests and difficulty reading as a child, I was created to find the gist of extensive processes due to my heavy right-brained development. This was a common dyslexic ability.

My tasks included research permit development, habitat conservation planning, critical habitat designation, and more. I was also part of a team responsible for adding and removing species from the Endangered Species Act list and developing protective regulations.

A recovery plan describes what must be done to recover and remove a species from the Endangered Species Act. It is a road map that explains what must occur for recovery. I was on the recovery planning team and helped develop the multi-species recovery plan for salmon and steelhead in the Central Valley, California.

I remember one of my first significant consultations involved a bridge. I worked hard to incorporate measures to reduce the acoustic impacts of pile driving on listed fish in the area. The consultation was finished, and I was excited to visit to see how construction was going. When I arrived, they were pounding piles with no agreed-upon sound attenuation buffers. The site had dozens of contractors, and it was a significant operation. I looked at the foreman and said, "Where are the bubble curtains and sound attenuation measures I require?" He said he was not aware. I then told him they needed to stop work immediately, and they did. They shut down and left. I referred the matter to law enforcement and the appropriate agencies, which delayed the project for months.

I returned to the office, complaining about what I had just witnessed. I soon learned this was a common problem. It was one thing to require many things in the consultation documents, but another to make sure they happened.

We had one law enforcement officer in the Central Valley at the time, and I partnered with him; we started visiting projects unannounced, which was exciting and uncomfortable at times. He carried a gun and badge; unlike me, he enjoyed getting into people's faces. When we found problems, he would turn to me and make me decide how bad it was in front of the construction crews.

The Endangered Species Act is nearly as old as I am. It is a groundbreaking and critical piece of legislation that will prevent the imminent extinction of species and the destruction of ecosystems on which they depend. Humans also rely on these ecosystems. I thoroughly enjoyed working as an endangered species consultation biologist for the National Marine Fisheries Service.

Chapter Seventeen

San Joaquin River Restoration Coordinator

When I was at the National Marine Fisheries Service, I was asked to apply for a promotion to a position at the U.S. Fish and Wildlife Service's regional office. As a general principle of mine, if I am asked to apply for a job, I seriously consider doing so, especially if the person doing the asking is doing the hiring! I applied, was interviewed, and was offered a position. This new position was a move from the Department of Commerce to the Department of Interior of the federal government.

Some months after starting my new position, I was asked to participate with the U.S. Bureau of Reclamation (Bureau) in developing guidance documents to set up the roles and responsibilities of a major restoration program. I worked closely with the Bureau, setting up a program management plan to lay out agency responsibilities for the new program. I was then asked to join the San Joaquin River Restoration Program office as the U.S. Fish and Wildlife Service representative. I transferred to a new position, working full-time for the restoration program.

It was interesting working closely with the Bureau, which had a completely different agency culture than the U.S. Fish and Wildlife Service. The Bureau's focus was water, which included the delivery of water and the infrastructural improvements to make the program happen. I represented the U.S. Fish and Wildlife Service and was to assist with completing the goal of restoring fish. These opposing goals created tension between the Bureau and other agency partners.

The Bureau person in charge of the San Joaquin River Restoration Program was also a Christian, and we connected on a new level. We became close, often discussing spiritual things and sharing our faith. He couldn't believe there was someone at the U.S. Fish and Wildlife Service who was a Christian. He thought the agency consisted of nothing but atheists and tree-huggers. He likely thought that about the agency as it is rare to talk about faith in the U.S. Fish and Wildlife Service. It is a science-based agency with individuals who typically believe the earth and everything in it can be explained by science. Faith involves beliefs that can challenge scientific beliefs, such as evolution. Due to a fear of exclusion, scientists in the agency typically avoid discussing matters of faith.

The San Joaquin River Restoration Program was one of the highest priorities of the Bureau at the time. I was exposed to a unique agency perspective because I worked in an office with all Bureau employees. I typically arrived at the office early because of my commute and would start the coffee pot. It just so happened that the Bureau Regional Director began his day early and would come by our office on his way in. The Regional Director heads thousands of employees and reports to Washington, DC. I would often be the only one there when he arrived, and we would talk. He would ask me questions regarding the fish side of things, and when I couldn't answer his questions, I would write them down.

As the restoration coordinator, I was responsible for administering and managing one of the country's most extensive fish restoration programs. I worked with the Bureau to organize efforts to complete the restoration aspects of the program. My focus was developing a fisheries management plan with a team of consultants and agencies. This document also contained a conceptual model of salmon, which was used to pinpoint scientific uncertainty and research needs.

The San Joaquin River Restoration Program was responsible for reintroducing salmon back to the river sixty years after its extinction. Our team had to gather research on salmon from nearby waterways and incorporate that information into conceptual models of their expected life history. We created a series of figures showing the exact process of each phase of the salmon life cycle. We incorporated scientific uncertainty into figures and accompanying text to inform future actions. For example, the conceptual model of the developing salmon eggs incorporated research around local sedimentation levels and spawning gravel availability. Salmon have particular gravel size requirements for adequate spawning and incubation. My prior research in the Delta was helpful, particularly when building the fry and juvenile conceptual models.

After the completion of the conceptual model, the fisheries management plan was built, laying out the framework for the reintroduction effort. I was the U.S. Fish and Wildlife Service representative of the team responsible for developing these documents. I was thankful for the assistance of several consultant teams in providing graphic and writing support. I spent so much time in one consultant's office that I felt I worked for them. Consultants have the flexibility the federal government does not have. For example, they knew I liked a particular brand of coffee, and they would always supply plenty for meetings, along with lunch and dessert. Sometimes, it is the simplest thing!

Both the negative and positive aspects of my dyslexia came out at this time. My intolerance of poorly organized documents shined brightly. Because I needed to understand the gist of an entire document first, I needed it to be organized well. I would often reject drafts of documents due to poor organization. Once the document was organized correctly, I could understand and dive into the details. I would usually get a quarter of the way into a document and reject it. I would refuse to read it until it was fixed and "readable." I believe this came across as perfectionism to some; however, I was the boss, and it was done. In the end, I thought the products were better.

I was fortunate to be invited to the Technical Advisory Committee for the San Joaquin River Restoration Program. This was a select group of hand-picked experts to oversee the implementation of the San Joaquin River Restoration Program. This group consisted of well-renowned salmon experts from academia and the consultant world. A Restoration Administrator led the Technical Advisory Committee, and we occasionally met in various West Coast locations for learning purposes. I remember once, I offered to drive the Restoration Administrator to a distant meeting. Everyone else had planned to arrive through separate means, and it was just the two of us. The only government vehicle available was this beat-up van with peeling paint. We got lost as we drove several hours away, joking about the van and whether we would make it. Not just a little lost. Very lost.

What could have been an unpleasant situation turned into a true blessing. We used the additional time to talk and get to know each other. We learned we had much more in common than we thought, and we bonded over things such as red wine, our Christian faith, and our families. We had a good working relationship due to that drive and my willingness to help.

There was a shortage of public affairs staff, and I was asked to lead the fish stakeholder group. This was not particularly pleasant, as scores of people didn't like the program and were attempting to slow it down with criticism. The tension and stress began to take its toll on me. My commute was more than an hour by car each way. I shifted my hours to avoid the brunt of the traffic; however, each day involved a stressful drive. In addition, the implementation of the restoration aspects of the program was highly controversial, creating a lot of pressure and stress.

I received a message from a colleague at the National Marine Fisheries Service that they were advertising a new position as the manager of the Central Valley Division. This position was second in charge of the Division and would be a promotion. I happily applied, was interviewed, and accepted this new opportunity, which would be my job for the next eight years. This position was closer to home than my current position so that I could shorten my commute considerably. In addition, several public transit options existed.

I tend to change jobs more frequently than most people. To make each departure more memorable, I would play a little prank. When leaving each position, I left a sealed envelope in the desk drawer marked "Confidential - Do Not Open". Inside the envelope was a sticky note that said something like, "Hey, why did you open the envelope? You were not supposed to. By the way, this is a joke." This little joke always made me smile as I imagined the curiosity and confusion it would cause anyone who found it.

Chapter Eighteen

Division Manager

The year was 2009, and we lived in a modest, three-bedroom home on a pie-shaped lot in Lodi. The neighborhood was getting old and filled with extra cars, boats, and campers, making it look unkept. This started to bother us. We noticed a house down the street appeared unkept, and cars were coming and going at all hours. The police arrested the inhabitants for selling drugs, and the house sat vacant for a long time; one of our friends mowed the lawn to keep it from getting out of control. I enjoyed our corner lot with extra space for a large backyard lawn and a vegetable garden. We had been there for approximately five years and became good friends with the neighbors on our right side. We often brought our lawn chairs to their driveway and talked during summer evenings. Sometimes, we would order pizza and eat dinner on the driveway. The house on our left side had a lot of junk in the driveway, and sometimes, the garage would be open. We could see that it was packed to the ceiling with junk. A man in his fifties was living there with his father. We used to talk with the father, and he was nice. Eventually, we heard the father was moved to a long-term care facility. We started noticing cars visiting the house at odd times. They would only stay for a few minutes and then leave. Then, one day, we saw strange things left on the house's side, such as plumbing supplies, soil, and containers. I walked over to the house with a neighbor, and we noticed the electricity was bypassed at the meter. This was a clue of illegal activity.

Eventually, it became apparent there was likely a marijuana-growing operation going on. We saw a pickup truck loaded with potting soil in front of the house. And then it was gone the next day. We saw large trash bags filled with plants removed exactly every thirty days. My family had a good connection with law enforcement, and we discussed this with our friend, a drug enforcement officer. He was set to raid the house and told us to be gone. He went to pull permits for the raid, and the local police said they would take care of it. Nothing happened.

It was time for us to move, and we decided to purchase a house in the country with some space. I had just accepted the job working for the National Marine Fisheries Service in downtown Sacramento, and our new home was a few minutes closer to Sacramento, nestled between vineyards. This home was fully landscaped on two-thirds of an acre, with expansive lawns, redwood trees, and an excellent vegetable garden. Various plants were in bloom, and the landscaping was spectacular. The house was built in 1937 and was remodeled several times. The pool in the back was attractive to the entire family. I remember thinking it was relaxing—birds chirping, the breeze flowing through the trees, until we moved in when I noticed all the weeds that needed to be pulled! My gardening excursions took hold as I worked to expand the vegetable garden and plant an orchard. I also removed a huge tree, making space for a pumpkin patch. Anne works out her stress by baking cookies, and I work out my stress on the riding lawn mower!

I started commuting on a bus that drove toward Sacramento from Stockton. It would stop in Lodi and would go straight toward the office. I left the house at 5:50 a.m. and arrived at the office at 7:00 a.m. The bus would depart outside the office at 4:35 p.m. I came home at about 5:55 p.m. This made for a nine-hour workday with a solid twelve-hour day from door to door. This was a challenging feat, five days per week. Occasionally, the bus was late, sometimes very late. They shifted bus drivers several times a year, and we would have to give them directions.

Once, on our way in the morning, I woke up from my typical snooze and noticed we were driving towards Lake

Tahoe, nearly in Auburn. We had passed Sacramento by more than thirty minutes. We hadn't even gotten off the freeway. I looked at the bus driver and said, "Hey, you missed Sacramento!" We all fell asleep, and the bus driver kept driving on the freeway. He promptly turned the bus around, and several of us had to explain each stop. Once, the bus pulled over on the way to work due to engine trouble. The bus driver got out to look at the engine. As we sat there, half asleep, I saw the bus driver running back into the bus. He shouted, "Everybody out! The bus is on fire!" We woke up quickly and got off the bus. The engine was on fire, and the bus driver extinguished it. It was a cold morning as we stood in the weeds on the side of the freeway. They sent another bus to pick us up.

For several years, I took Amtrak. The train was an enjoyable method of commuting. First, it was a smooth ride with Wi-Fi and desk surfaces to work. Second, it went straight to downtown Sacramento, with no stops on the way. The problem? It was frequently late. When I say late, I mean hours late. It would also stop for no apparent reason. Train delays are significant.

Driving to the office was tiring due to the stress of navigating the freeway during rush hour and the poor parking situation. All commuting methods had downsides, and I had to tolerate the commute or move. I tried to make the best use of the commute time by reading books. Nevertheless, it was hard on my family and hard on me.

I started my position at the National Marine Fisheries Service during a highly turbulent time. I learned the office was on the precipice of moving between floors in the building. The office was expanding, and more space was needed.

Shortly before moving, my boss informed me she would take an extended leave for personal reasons. I had successfully ordered the office portion of the furniture, but it had yet to arrive. My boss had no time to pack, and guess who got to move her out? I had to go through her desk, files, and bookshelves and pack the materials. I even found a forgotten envelope with cash collected for an office party. I was able to use it to purchase pizza for the office!

It was time to move to the new space, and we weren't completely ready. Out of approximately fifty staff, I had space for about fifteen. Then, I had to procure the modular furniture and wait for delivery and installation. That furniture took forever to arrive. I rented large tables for desks, and we lined them up like a bingo hall in the workspace. This worked, but people were not accustomed to the lack of privacy. I got complaints about noise, private space, and even glare off the desks. At least we had lots of windows and natural light!

My office was enormous, decked out with fine wood furniture and two entire walls of windows. I overlooked the street leading to the state capital and could see all sorts of protests. Once, I saw a protest aimed at us. They were waving dead salmon and protesting changes to fishing regulations. Several times, protests became violent, and once they were able to enter the lobby of our building. It was always interesting to figure out what the protests were about.

Anne and I continued to make running a part of our daily routine, and we usually did so three to four times a week, even when I was commuting to Sacramento. We would wake up early to run in the neighborhood before sunrise. This time together became a habit and set a positive tone for the rest of our day. However, it's essential to note that running can come with certain risks.

We had a paper delivery person who delivered newspapers by car. Nowadays, this method of delivery is more frequent than bike delivery. We often saw the delivery car in the early morning while running on the road. Whenever we noticed the car approaching, we quickly moved to the shoulder of the street to let it pass. I remember several occasions when the driver passed us very closely on the wrong side of the road. Once, I felt the air brush as the car passed, and I don't think the driver even saw us. In retrospect, I should have paid more attention to these danger signals.

Anne and I were jogging about a half-mile from our house one morning. We noticed the familiar lights of the newspaper delivery person behind us. We moved to the side of the road to let them pass. The next thing I remember is the feeling of being thrown onto the gravel. I remember the gravel coming at my head quickly, and I had my hands in front of me. It happened so fast that it felt surreal. I also heard a thud and a bang and Anne shouting. The truck delivering the papers hit Anne first, striking her on the shoulder and pushing her to the side. Although Anne twisted and shouted, she managed to stay on her feet. Meanwhile, the rearview mirror hit me on my elbow, pushing me forward.

After I stopped sliding along the shoulder of the road, I lifted my head and saw the truck's brake lights that had hit us several hundred feet away. Amazed I was alive, I quickly got up and said, "I am okay" several times. We moved to the other side of the road and called 911. After 45 minutes, the police arrived. They went to the wrong city!

I declined an ambulance despite the officer's suggestions. I recall being confused about which direction home was, and Anne had to remind me. I was in a rush to get home to stay on schedule. Initially, I thought I could cover the wounds and still go to work. However, after examining the wounds, we both agreed that it would be best for me to stay home and seek medical attention.

I phoned the office to inform them that I wouldn't be able to come in because I got hit by a car while I was running. Unfortunately, I couldn't speak to anyone, so I left several voicemails. However, when I showed up to work the next day, I discovered that my colleagues had received my voicemails but were very concerned as they didn't know my condition.

That morning, I went to Kaiser to get checked out. It seemed like I had only suffered a broken thumb, some cuts, and bruises and didn't have any significant injuries. However, I may have had a concussion. On the other hand, Anne was not as lucky. She experienced weakness in her right shoulder that lasted for a long time. After more than a year of physical therapy appointments, she finally appeared to have healed.

Individuals with dyslexia often exhibit a remarkable ability to navigate situations involving many unknown variables and rapid changes. Moreover, they excel at developing innovative and creative solutions for complex problems. I faced a challenging situation when my boss returned from leave and informed me that the two regions on the West Coast would be merging. Such an event brought unprecedented change and uncertainty for me as a federal employee. It is worth noting that all mergers, splits, and reorganizations come with their own set of winners and losers and take considerable time to finalize.

My job changed rapidly as the region merged and the various executives formed committees. I began working with a new group of West Coast managers to move the new region's administrative and management aspects forward. I was a founding member of the Division Manager team. Some people shut down during the uncertainty of the situation, resisting the change. I fit in well during the uncertainty and exploration of new roles and tasks. I jumped right into strategic discussions and the details of processes. However, being a big-picture thinker does come with risks. I occasionally moved ahead of the group, overlooking details and processes as I suggested new ideas. Some ideas would be too outside the box or at least too far ahead of the discussions. This would cause people to become frustrated as I appeared too abstract. I would need to be brought back to reality by the group. I would toss out many potential ideas, some of which would stick. So, I had to make my big-picture comments carefully.

I continued to use my creativity skills to solve complex workflow problems. I worked on a standard, repeatable budgeting process each year and for each office. Hiring was a considerable time sink, and we worked on streamlining it. I established a work distribution method and acquired contracting staff to support the Division.

Research on people with dyslexia reveals they are good at finding the central idea of things. I discussed my ability to get to the gist of documents and extensive processes. I was often tasked with responding to letters from Congress and external parties addressed to our agency. Usually, these letters would come to our office by way of

Washington, DC, and they would be filled with inaccurate interpretations and political rhetoric. I worked with senior leadership to write letters back. I also reviewed and approved regulations and notices before publication in the Federal Register. Topics included critical habitat designations, listing determinations, protective regulations, and experimental population designations. Complex biological analysis, policy development, and Congressional correspondence used my right-brained skills well to focus on the essential aspects of these tasks rather than go down rabbit trails into details.

One of the other supervisors was also a Christian. Despite our busy schedules, we always discussed church, faith, and family. We discovered two other coworkers were also Christian, and we had four people, enough people for a Bible study. Federal rules prohibit operating a Bible study during business hours, and as supervisors, we were forbidden from announcing a Bible study with government computers. None of us were comfortable sharing with our co-workers that we were Christian out of fear we would be judged or, worse, retaliated against in some way by management. It was unfortunate to feel this way. In an agency that prides itself on embracing diversity, we feared discussing our Christian faith. So, we met during lunchtime in a private conference room once a week. I felt like we were in the underground church!

The challenge of breaking down a complex issue that involves culture, science, policy, government, and natural resources can be relished by a person with dyslexia. One such challenge came my way while working with the Winnemem Wintu Native American tribe. They were located along the McCloud River, and they caught wind that my agency was considering the reintroduction of salmon to a watershed running through their land. I met with the tribe in Sacramento to discuss the effort. They were against the project and wanted to film the meeting for later use. This was against our policy, and the first part of the meeting was convincing the videographer to turn off the video. We then discussed the potential project, and I learned they were against it as they believed we would be introducing the wrong fish. They had a connection with the native fish of the McCloud River, but unfortunately, these fish were no longer in the river due to dams. However, before the fish disappeared, a batch of the eggs was taken to New Zealand, where a thriving salmon fishery existed.

The Winnemem Wintu tribe visited New Zealand and indicated that the fish came up and talked to them, telling them they wanted to go home. I assured them that the fish we would introduce would be genetically pure. However, they would hear none of that. They wanted fish from New Zealand. As commonly observed in people with dyslexia, I was particularly good at seeing connections and relationships of cultures, particularly in this case, as the Winnemem Wintu tribe often talked through stories. Stories significantly impact me as I learn best in this manner. Happily, progress appears to be made, and the tribe and the agency are planning the introduction approximately twelve years after that meeting.

People with dyslexia may exhibit a slower response time. I, too, experience occasional delays and find verbal and written questions challenging. Complex inquiries take me a day or more to formulate a response. I spontaneously enter someone's office multiple times weekly, exclaiming, "I just thought of a response to that issue this morning." The early morning hours often spark creative ideas for me.

Once, I got a chilling phone call. I was the only manager in the office at the time, so I picked up my phone. The person said, "Is this Jeff McLain?" I responded, "Yes, how can I help you?" He explained that he immediately needed some answers to some local fish questions. He was communicating through an earpiece to a Department of Commerce official on stage giving a speech. The first question was, "Is there monitoring for sturgeon in that area?" I answered, stating there was monitoring happening. He said, "One moment...waiting for questions." Next question, "Who does this monitoring, and what type is it?" I answered confidently, and again, I got the "One moment...waiting for questions." Then he said there were no further questions, thanked me for my service, and hung up. Silly me, I forgot to ask his name. I searched the news and all potential political speech locations and found nothing. I did not have time to come up with a response in this instance. When I am pressured to answer immediately in such cases, I often second-guess my responses. I would prefer to have ample time to digest a topic.

I mentioned my strong ability to empathize with others. I especially have a lot of empathy for others who have been treated poorly. One of our best employees in the office was a Black veteran. He proved invaluable to the agency, demonstrating exceptional dedication and a solid commitment to service. As I got to know him, I learned about the struggles with discrimination he dealt with frequently. It was not uncommon for him to be shown disrespect for no apparent reason or to be looked over due to his skin color. I found out that all staff in his position in the region were recently promoted. Everyone except him. How could an agency do that to a person? I proceeded to promote him immediately.

I observed a supervisor fixated on a particular employee or group multiple times. This narrow focus caused them to take a short-term approach to problem-solving, which was understandable at the moment. However, as someone with a broader perspective of the entire office, I could concentrate on the big picture rather than getting lost in the details. An office's workforce is a complex system, and I have honed my ability to detect patterns and identify trends in such situations.

I noticed a variety of work ethics and abilities. Most staff members were competent, hardworking individuals. Some were hardworking and not as skilled; however, they worked hard and made up for it. A small percentage didn't appear to do as much. They seemed to suffer from incompetence and a lack of motivation or work ethic. These staff tended to take time from others by causing problems. Others would have to finish their work when they missed deadlines, and their writing was so poor that they went through countless edits, taking others' valuable time. These low performers typically survived in the system for a long time, as they could not find other jobs, and their supervisors continued to try to improve their performance without success. They typically wouldn't receive merit pay raises or awards and would become disgruntled. In some cases, they had been given awards in the past to avoid complaints and potentially improve their morale, but this rarely worked in the long run. Addressing performance concerns in the biological sciences was challenging and seldom practical due to the lack of a measurable deliverables system for developing an improvement plan.

The overwhelming majority of staff were extremely hardworking public servants, many working so many hours in front of deadlines that they wouldn't record their time.

Countless hours were donated, and significant stress was incurred to meet deadlines. I was awed and inspired frequently.

My capacity for empathy and warmth was often needed to work with staff negotiating work and life problems. For example, if an employee exhibited poor performance or conduct problems, I would first seek to understand what was happening. Before jumping to discipline, I would meet with the employee and ask if things were okay. Commonly, the employee was struggling with a problem outside of work and needed support and time. As a supervisor, I always strived to give employees as much understanding as possible and give them the benefit of the doubt.

Chapter Nineteen

Church

My mother-in-law was diagnosed with pancreatic cancer in 2008. She vowed to fight it, and we all prayed and kept our hopes up. Several complications occurred, and doctors were unable to get the disease under control. She fought the disease for nearly a year—a massive feat for pancreatic cancer. I remember visiting while my father-in-law was taking care of her at the house when she was in hospice. The rock-solid Christian grandma and mother of my wife was withering away, and it was heartbreaking. We lost her in September 2009. It isn't easy to understand why a good person suffers and passes early. We get confused when we pray for months and years for healing, and it doesn't happen. I will never have all the answers, but God needed her elsewhere. She was healed, just not here on earth.

I no longer spent extra hours at work or the gym on nights and weekends and shifted more time to be with family and church. I was nominated and then voted to the church elder board for the first time in 2010, and continued to serve in this manner as chair, secretary, and board member for the past 14 years. The board is the governing body of our church and works with the senior pastor to lead the church. Typical tasks include vision, prayer, budgeting, dispute resolution, and teaching. Many of the skills I developed in the workplace were helpful to the church—for example, workforce management, human resources, and administrative processes.

The elder board of my church consists of approximately twelve men who meet the biblical qualifications of an elder. These qualifications, outlined in the Bible, include traits such as being free from the love of money, possessing gentleness, exhibiting respectability, and being adept at teaching the gospel. Board members encompass a diverse range of professions, including company presidents, CEOs, former and current pastors, and business leaders. This group operates with deep insight and fervent prayer, prioritizing Jesus at the forefront of their decisions.

Serving on the elder board provides valuable lessons transferable to the workplace. Like management positions, board service can be challenging, acknowledging that even churches encounter issues. Both churches and workplaces consist of people who each have complex challenges. However, in the church situation, the power of prayer is revealed, and I get to see God's work amid the challenges.

I recall numerous instances where prayers were fervently offered and answered at the eleventh hour. One poignant example involves a friend battling severe cancer, with the entire men's ministry of the church consistently praying for him. The church community went above and beyond, supporting the family by taking care of his kids, providing meals, and offering various forms of assistance. I distinctly remember gathering in large groups for collective prayers, especially when his condition became critical, and plans for his family's future were being considered. On a pivotal morning, as he faced a crucial doctor's appointment, many men from the church surprised him by encircling his house, joining hands, and praying for his healing. Astonishingly, that day's appointment did not revolve around planning for his end; the doctor, unable to explain it, confirmed the inexplicable disappearance of the cancer. While I have witnessed miraculous healings, I've also encountered instances where, despite fervent prayers, people passed away prematurely. The mystery of life and death remains, and we grapple with unanswered questions.

Lives are changed continually through recovery programs and Bible studies. Marriages are repaired, members kick drug habits and addictions, and alcoholics recover. The church is full of broken, sinful people trying to do better—and the church is in the business of repairing people.

When I walk through the church's doors, I feel the Holy Spirit. It is a warmth and comfort. Often, thoughts come into my head, mostly during worship. They are ideas or answers to significant challenges I am faced with at the time. I have come to learn that this is the Holy Spirit. The Holy Spirit is a true gift from God.

Chapter Twenty

Servant Leadership

Over my thirty years of working for the government, I have witnessed democratic leadership, laissez-faire leadership, authoritative leadership, and just about everything in between. My leadership style combines leadership qualities I have seen and my own goals and personality. I was blessed to have a coach who provided leadership support while I worked at the National Marine Fisheries Service. We would talk frequently about leadership styles, organizational topics, visioning, and retreats. This coach had assisted past government executives and various CEOs. After I described my goals and leadership style, the coach said he thought I sounded like a servant leader.

In the business world, servant leadership was coined by Robert K. Greenleaf in a 1970 essay, *The Servant as Leader*. Greenleaf was a Christian and eventually converted to

Quakerism, and I can only assume the Bible influenced his definition of servant leadership. The premise of servant leadership is that leaders should help others, and true servants operate out of love. A critical component of servant leaders is compassionately empathizing with others. While it would appear servants aren't truly leaders, as they are in the mode of doing things for others, it is not so. True leaders seek to help others and lift them up. Servant leaders put others first, and in so doing, they lead.

11*The greatest among you shall be your servant.* (Matthew 23:11, The Holy Bible, NIV).

Jesus articulated the importance of servant leadership over 2,000 years ago, setting the ultimate example by sacrificing his life for all humanity. The Bible is full of references to being a servant, not only at work but at church, to the poor, and in everyday life. As my servant leadership style continued to emerge at the National Marine Fisheries Service, it became clear it was paradoxically opposite to that of many leaders in the agency at the time. While I strived to help others, including my boss, and to put others first, many leaders put themselves first. These leaders were more defined as authoritarian or power leaders. These leaders used power in their positions as their primary motivators. It was their way or the highway. Teams and meetings were often used to report back to the power leader. The power leader then issued tasks and demands and loved to take credit for other people's work. It is not uncommon for a general fear and low morale to develop under a power leader, as the business relationship becomes impersonal, stressful, and intimidating. I think there is a place for servant leaders and a place for power leaders, and both types are in many businesses and agencies. The servant leader is prone to doing too much and helping too much. The power leader delegates well and is not prone to taking on too much. In my opinion, a combination can be beneficial; however, if the power leader is the dominant style, low morale and high turnover are to be expected.

Here is an example of servant leadership. I realized that my team had significant talent that could be useful for my important presentation to upper management. Although I had some ideas about what to say, I understood that others would be better at the presentation. Therefore, I asked one of our junior staff members for assistance, and they did a fantastic job developing the slides. After completing the presentation, I informed the officials that I had help putting it together and that the work was not mine but that of a staff member I mentioned by name. The staff member who did the presentation felt a sense of accomplishment and was recognized for their work. As a result, I started a coaching and mentoring relationship with the staff person as I continued to support and guide them.

In light of these experiences, I propose that employees with a moral compass are of tremendous value to government agencies. In my case, the Bible provides all the answers and guidance I need. It is based on the perfect wisdom of God. I am not trusting solely in my judgment to do what is right and wrong but also in the morals God created. We are faced with many decisions and dilemmas, and our feelings get in the way, as well as our pride and selfishness. Thus, it is easy to justify incorrect decisions when one sets their morals on their desires and judgment. Some people get it right, and their morals match the government's needs; however, plenty get it wrong.

Chapter Twenty-One

Giant Pumpkins

Since childhood, a lesson ingrained in me has been the pursuit of hobbies—an activity highly endorsed for children with dyslexia. Embracing this practice in my youth, I continue to derive benefit from it to this day. When one enters the professional world and the stresses of work begin to creep in, hobbies are a great way to relax your mind. Hobbies and outdoor activities contribute to my resilience and are key to my work longevity. Aquarium fish, weightlifting, fort building, and sports motivated me and built my self-esteem in my youth. Now, my hobbies seem more focused on gardening and growing giant pumpkins, and they help lower my work stress.

When Anne and I moved to our second house in the early 2000s, we had room for a vegetable garden. Living in the Central Valley, we were surrounded by agriculture but didn't know how to start. Fortunately for us, Anne's Uncle

Norman was a farmer and an inspiring tutor. I asked Norman for some help, and he became my gardening mentor. Norman took me to Lockhart Seeds in Stockton, where they sold hundreds of seeds for commercial and residential farming. We were in that store for hours as Norman showed me seed types, bulbs, tubers, fertilizers, and everything else. He gave me detailed growing instructions, and my first vegetable garden was a success thanks to him.

Norman had grown plants commercially for many years and was filled with knowledge. Some foods he grew were citrus fruits, grapes, cantaloupe, and almonds. Once, I needed help understanding how to harvest melons. I called Norman, and he explained the specifics of melon maturation. Norman's depth of knowledge about fruit and vegetable growing always amazed me. Norman also grew vegetables as a kid, entering them in fairs and contests. He was particularly fond of onions. More than once, I called him to ask some onion questions, and he would talk for nearly an hour about them. Unfortunately, Lockhart Seeds has closed, and I get my seeds on the internet now. My dear gardening mentor and friend Norman passed away in early 2023.

In 2016, I made a bet with a friend that I could grow a more enormous pumpkin than him. My friend had just moved to a new home, and he had space to grow a pumpkin, and I had a big yard. The bet was on, and I ordered giant pumpkin seeds from an online retailer. We went our separate ways and scoured the internet for giant pumpkin-growing tips. We purchased our fertilizers and checked with all experts known to us. I was unaware at the time that my friend's uncle was a legitimate giant pumpkin grower and was offering advice to him. As our first season progressed, we noticed our giant pumpkins were more like white squash. They ended at about thirty-five pounds each, and we called it a draw—although I think my friend's pumpkin was slightly larger.

My friend secured some legitimate pumpkin seeds from a 900-pound pumpkin the following year. He could not grow a giant in his backyard but gave me seeds. That year, I grew an 800-pounder in my backyard and was permanently hooked on growing giant pumpkins. I was super excited about it at work and shared it with everyone. They all got behind me and asked me continuously about the pumpkin as it was growing. In the following years, I continued to grow pumpkins and took them to sanctioned weigh-offs. Unlike my former powerlifting days when I tried to lift a lot of weight, I was now trying to grow a lot of weight! I achieved some success, taking home some prize money.

To grow a pumpkin, all one needs to do is basic gardening. However, much knowledge and skill are required to produce a true giant. Like anything else, the more you get into something, the more you learn. As I tried new approaches each year, I would take notes. My notes turned into chapters, and I had the basics of a book. In 2022, I published *Backyard Big: Growing Atlantic Giant Pumpkins in Your Backyard*, my first book. I dedicated my book to Norman, my gardening mentor. We had a memorable conversation about the book before he passed away. I was inspired to start my business, *Jeffslodigarden*, selling pumpkin seeds, my book, and other gardening-related items. My sales are used to purchase fertilizers and supplies for my growing. This hobby and new business have allowed me to envision what I will do in my retirement years.

Chapter Twenty-Two

Management

P rayer is an interesting thing. We pray for healing, well-being, peace, safety, and more. We anticipate that our prayers will be answered, and, in many cases, they are; however, they are only sometimes answered in our timing or the way we think they should be. There are also times when that prayer is answered precisely as we wanted.

In 2015, I was praying for a long list of requests, including the health of various family members and friends, cancer cures, and a job opening for me closer to home. Occasionally, I make lists so I don't forget to pray for particular people. I put the list away in my junk drawer and found it several years later. I had discovered that many of the prayers were answered with a YES. Some were answered differently. Some people passed on, and some things didn't work out from my perspective. It turned out that my prayer for work closer to home would come true.

In 2018, I was notified by an employee at the U.S. Fish and Wildlife Service that a permanent GS-14 position was advertised at an office a mere four miles from my house. This was the same office I'd worked in when I started my career in 1992. Could this be one of my prayers answered? I was encouraged to apply and took this notification seriously. I applied for the position and forwarded my information to the hiring official. I interviewed with a team of senior leaders from several agencies and thought I did horribly. The questions were tough, and I left the interview feeling I had bombed it. I was offered the position with a salary at a GS-14, step 10 level several days later and happily accepted. I was to earn the maximum wage a non-politically appointed civilian employee could make in the agency. I was told the interview was intentionally challenging to sort out the crowd.

This new position was entirely different than all the positions I'd held in the past. It was the top position in a vast office. Rather than working for programs, such as a restoration program or a program related to a specific fish species, I was responsible for an office implementing many programs. The skills required for this opportunity involved assessing and changing the organizational structure, improving the efficiency of the office as a whole, and rooting out things impacting morale. With over eighty staff, the office was one of the largest field offices in the United States.

It is common for individuals with dyslexia to prefer diagrams, charts, and figures versus a written narrative to learn a topic. I depend on visual images to understand and learn. I routinely use scratch paper to sketch processes to improve my understanding. Sequences, relationships, and topics are described with flow charts and diagrams I draw on scratch paper. I will often read a narrative description of a process and grab a piece of paper to create a visual image of the narrative. I commonly bring my sketches to others to ensure I understand the processes correctly. This is extremely helpful, as images and not words are my primary language in understanding complex processes. Doing this gives me a different perspective than my nondyslexic colleagues.

I started my understanding of the office with the organization chart. The first chart I looked at needed so much work I decided to toss it and start over. One of the first tasks I delegated to staff was the creation of a new organizational chart, showing levels and groupings of the office to understand workflow and communication. Many staff were functioning without a clear understanding of the organizational structure. I couldn't move on without a thorough assessment. I needed to "get on the balcony" to see the office from the big-picture perspective. I had just moved into the position, and the timing for this work was perfect. I observed communication between staff and teams of the various office groups. The regional office also asked me to investigate the morale of the office and see what was going on, as it was consistently rated the lowest in the country per federal surveys. It was time for me to use my communication, listening, and empathy to figure out what was happening.

First, the office space was approximately half the size it should have been and needed more space for all staff. It had been suffering from this problem for at least a decade. As programs were added and expanded, and more staff were added, additional workspace was not. Small desks were purchased and put in corners and hallways to compensate for this. These were used as office space and assumed to be a regular part of the office. This wasn't enough extra space, as the office was still short of more than twenty spaces for staff. Fairness was lacking; some staff were assigned cubicles, others were relegated to small corner desks, and some were left without a workspace. Inequality often correlated with seniority, where prolonged tenure allowed the acquisition of a workspace.

Second, the nature of the work in the office depended on the heavy use of entry-level temporary staff. There needed to be more room for upward advancement, and many staff would leave as soon as they found permanent work elsewhere. This caused frequent employee shortages and near-constant hiring, as staff would leave for advancement opportunities. Low salaries, high turnover, and a temporary nature worsened the situation, forcing many to survive on meager wages. It was common for coworkers to rent houses or apartments together to save money. All this made for a sour recipe at times, as work would blend into personal life and vice-versa, creating alliances, opposing groups, and nepotism situations. For some, work was a happy place with acceptance and belonging. For others, it was toxic.

The mechanic and boat operators managed an extensive field operation, including over 30 research vessels, 20 vehicles, and various tools. Over time, the operation grew, and they faced challenges in organizing and managing it effectively. While expensive tools valued over $5,000 were part of the federal inventory system, cheaper hand tools were scattered across different vehicles, vessels, and the warehouse, making tracking difficult. As a result, it was easier to purchase a new tool than to find one. This was not an efficient use of resources.

Finally, the administrative team was the size it always had been—five or six people. Yet the office size, processes, paperwork requirements, and tasks had increased exponentially over the years. Administrative staff were underpaid and burned out. Efficiency and formal policy revisions were needed to keep up with the growing office.

My immediate priorities included restructuring the office to break down alliances and divisions, improve communication, expand the workspace, streamline administrative processes, create advancement and detail opportunities, and develop a mentoring program. These were the high-level items I focused on, and I continued to try to improve many other areas of the office, such as supervision and budgeting.

To address the tool and equipment accountability challenge, I spearheaded the development of a robust inventory system. Fortunately, some of our staff members had prior equipment inventory experience from their military time. Leveraging their expertise, we devised a system that utilized barcodes to meticulously track the location of tools and equipment, ensuring efficient management and accountability.

Another change that I made, which was in line with my personality, was to step out of my office and play a more active role in office and field leadership. By simply walking around and connecting with people, I noticed an improvement in morale across all levels. Regular personal interaction facilitated better communication and made relationships less formal. Additionally, a warm smile helped build trust and fostered psychological safety.

A particular weakness of mine is memorizing rules and protocols, a common dyslexic challenge. I learn the rules best by experiencing them; if I don't experience them, it is difficult to commit them to memory. Thus, much of my time is spent reviewing the rules and policies. Fortunately, I have excellent staff with more rules on the tip of their tongue than I had in my head.

Taking over an office means inheriting its successes and shortcomings that may have persisted for decades. While some issues are immediately apparent, others surface over time. Flawed processes and inadequate planning can become deeply rooted in operations, making them resistant to change. Positive transformations require a leader to display courage and determination, which can sometimes feel isolating.

You also get to inherit a legacy of good things. The office had more than its share of issues but was amazingly productive in a few areas. The office had acquired numerous experts in fish biology and statistics, resulting in several highly influential peer-reviewed publications and biological models used by government agencies and academia. In addition, the office continued to provide high-quality fish catch information and completed significant salmon restoration projects.

I prioritized the needs of others and introduced a culture of empathy and mutual support in the office. I started resume workshops, mock interviews, and other support efforts, which improved morale and culture. Additionally, staff felt supported and saw advancement opportunities in the office and beyond.

Instead of a vacation in 2019, my family decided to go on a mission trip to a small town in Mexico. We went to a youth camp to help the local community in an impoverished area. We did light construction, painted, fed people experiencing poverty, and helped kids with sports. We stayed in the facility but ate in families' homes, which was terrific. We also helped a youth center in a nearby town and ate in the mayor's house most days.

One night, we were invited to dinner and were challenged to a karaoke sing-off, complete with tequila. As the night unfolded, the rivalry intensified with each round. Fortunately, a church choir member was with us, and we could hold our own. Sadly, we had to leave for the airport in the morning and declined offers to stay up singing. They were so gracious and welcoming.

Several months later, I took two pastors to the area to introduce them to the mission effort. After that, our church funded the start-up of a Christian church in the area. Nobody at work knew where I went and what I did during those two trips.

Chapter Twenty-Three

COVID-19

Adaptive leadership is a leadership practice that responds and adapts to change. It offers particular tools that help the leader react in times of uncertainty through experiences. As situations shift in uncertain directions, adaptive leaders learn and evolve. In my opinion, individuals with dyslexia are built to implement adaptive leadership. Their minds are structured to learn through adaptation, experience, and testing.

I have worked for the federal government for over thirty years and have experienced many disruptions, including furloughs, lousy budget years, and political interference. Without question, the most significant event in my career was the COVID-19 pandemic. The pandemic was brutal on everyone and especially hard on my current U.S. Fish and Wildlife Service office, as much of the office was required to work through the pandemic in the field using boats and vehicles. I depended on my adaptive leadership skills to persevere through the COVID-19 pandemic.

When COVID-19 first reached our county and people began getting sick, little was known about how it spread, and mortality rates were relatively high. It was determined that our office would continue to work in the field through COVID-19. We were told to continue working, as fish-catch information was needed for water use purposes in California. We continued striving to prioritize safety, but all my staff got the message that work was number one and safety was number two. As government offices sent staff home in our state, our office was required to perform critical fieldwork.

In late March 2020, our first employee fell ill with COVID-19. There was a high level of tension among the field staff, and morale was so low for a time that I was concerned I would have a mutiny on my hands. Supervisors would get early-morning calls from staff in tears when they were not feeling well, fearing they would become seriously ill or even die. Several employees left the agency with no job. They just gave up. The field crew felt they risked their health for their work. Meanwhile, most members of government agencies went home and teleworked. I was forced to send my staff into the field, and the message they got was that they were sacrificed.

Our office quickly pivoted and acquired laptops so many could work from home when not in the field or exposed to COVID-19. Positions routinely not eligible for telework became eligible. Boat operators took nets home and repaired them in their backyards. When employees were exposed to COVID-19, our supervisors referred to a compiled list of potential tasks, and the employees were assigned specific responsibilities to complete at home.

Because of the pandemic, boat parts became scarce, engines were difficult to acquire, and service shops were backed up. This required creative and innovative methods of fixing boats and staying on the water. Engines were cannibalized from other boats, and parts were acquired quickly once discovered to be available.

Oral communication is a strength of mine, and this is a common dyslexic trait. I hosted daily staff meetings to inform everyone of changing policies and how to adjust. Adjustments related to infection control, physical distancing requirements, and other aspects were ongoing. Shifts started staggered, transportation shifted to single occupancy vehicles, and masks were required in the field on boats. I actively reached out to our employee assistance program for help with both my guilt about sending staff into the field and how to handle things. I recall having an all-hands call with the Regional Director to discuss our concerns. I cried in front of the Regional Director and all my staff. This was not normal for me.

To ensure continued operations and prevent the spread of the virus, we enlisted a company specializing in cleaning and sanitizing office surfaces. Notably, they employed electrostatic fogging equipment—a method utilizing an electrostatic sprayer to apply a charged disinfectant mist. Widely used in healthcare facilities, schools, and public spaces, this method helps mitigate the transmission of pathogens. Not only was it challenging to schedule the services of this company due to high demand, but it was costly.

Inspired by this approach, one of our staff members developed a COVID-19 prevention program. This initiative responded swiftly to potential sickness or exposure events, triggering immediate decontamination measures. Staff received prompt notifications, and our dedicated electrostatic fogging equipment was deployed to sanitize field equipment, boats, vehicles, the office, and the warehouse. Exposed staff were sent home, and the entire office was sometimes temporarily closed.

As the understanding of COVID-19 transmission evolved, it became evident that the virus primarily spreads through the air. Consequently, the emphasis on the fogging program decreased. Nevertheless, I take pride in reporting that staff-to-staff transmission of COVID-19 remained exceptionally low due to our proactive measures. Electrostatic fogging continues to be implemented during the flu and cold seasons.

I attempted to purchase vaccinations for our staff, particularly field workers, but it was impossible. Eventually, vaccinations became available throughout the county, and all our staff were eligible at the same time as the teleworkers and everyone else in the county. I don't need to explain the impact of this on morale. It is just the way it happened.

I lost a friend to COVID-19. Several weeks after I talked with him, he passed away after a rough battle in the hospital. Many in my community were lost. My wife was forced to return to school to teach third grade, and she and all the students were required to wear masks for months. My two children did high school online at home for a year. Then, they went back to school in masks. My wife and both my children caught COVID-19, presumably at school.

On May 25, 2020, America was horrified when a video of the murder of a Black man by white police officers in Minnesota surfaced in the media. One officer had hand-cuffed and pinned George Floyd to the ground, using the force of a knee on his neck. The video showed Floyd's more than nine-minute ordeal and his continual cries for relief so he could breathe. Officers nearby did nothing to stop the brutal murder. Everyone was reminded of the serious problem of police brutality and racism in our country. Once again, I was confronted with issues I never imagined I would need to deal with at work. Many staff members were disgusted and moved to action. But what could be done for federal employees?

As an office, The only saving grace was that we had a way to process this murder together, as we had become accustomed to having frequent all-hands meetings several times a week during COVID-19. Our agency, including our regional office, sent strong messages about the need to address racial discrimination and violence.

Injustice is wrong, and loving everyone equally is a significant value. Furthermore, the encouragement of diversity demonstrates empathy and is a critical servant leader skill—so important that Jesus himself mentioned it when asked about the greatest commandment.

37Jesus replied: 'Love the Lord your God with all your heart and with all your soul and with all your mind.' 38This is the first and greatest commandment. 39And the second is like it: 'Love your neighbor as yourself.' (Matthew 22:37-39, Holy Bible, NIV)

Both these essential values are easily transferred to a work environment. We are not to judge, and we are to love everyone equally. I have accepted this command and live it out at work. I regularly pray for employees at my office. I pray for specific employees when I feel the need and also pray for the entire office regularly. Does my staff realize this?

It took many months, but some solutions were emerging to respond to the murder of George Floyd. Many of us agreed that something must be done, and the time for talk was over. Yet, our agency and the policies and structure restricted many options. For example, we inquired with our managers about the possibility of reading a book about racial injustice together as an office, and we were sternly warned against doing such a thing as it could create too much of a stir.

Then, a recommendation from a staff member was made to develop a diversity and inclusion team. The voluntary team was a welcome new activity that provided a safe place to talk and grieve together. The team started to look internally at hiring and office practices to provide recommendations to management about making changes to incorporate diversity and inclusion principles. The diversity and inclusion team has helped organize and distribute office-wide informational emails and postings about various diversity and inclusion topics. They also provide valuable hiring feedback. This team was a positive addition following a cruel murder—another example of a terrible situation with a silver lining. I decided not to be threatened by the diversity and inclusion team but to partner with them and take advantage of their creativity and leadership.

To make matters worse, the California wildfires raged in the fall of 2020, and the air was unhealthy in the Central Valley of California. We developed a new air quality index protocol, and the field crew had to deal with excessive heat, COVID-19, and poor air quality. Of course, the masks used for COVID-19 on the boats were unsuitable for wildfire smoke, and they had to be upgraded. Many sampling days were lost due to severe air quality problems.

I am part of a Christian accountability group that gathers weekly for breakfast. In our meetings, we engage in Bible studies, read books collectively, participate in service projects, offer mutual support, share in moments of grief, and occasionally organize family events together. I look forward to the conversations, prayer, and encouragement weekly. Following our prayer, each breakfast usually incorporates a Bible study topic. Our talks are actually about mutual encouragement and accountability. There are five others in this group: a school counselor, a physician, a business entrepreneur, a pastor, a physiology professor, and a researcher. I have met every Thursday at 6:00 a.m. for breakfast with this group for nearly twenty years. We have switched breakfast locations numerous times for a variety of reasons. Sometimes, the food changes and becomes poor; it is the coffee. We befriend the staff wherever we are, tipping them heavily and praying for them. This group's support, encouragement, and accountability have been such a blessing over the years. They have lifted me up during difficult times and celebrated with me during the good times. In addition, I often bring my spiritual questions to this group, and we frequently get into deep spiritual topics. We have hiked to the top of Half Dome in Yosemite National Park three times and continue talking about new adventures. As we get older, we are considering hiking adventures of a less rigorous nature. I love doing life with these guys!

We could not meet for breakfast regularly at the beginning of the COVID-19 pandemic as most restaurants closed. We met in backyards when we could, but we missed a lot of breakfasts, making the pandemic even more challenging to navigate without help from my group. In addition, the church was going through changes and trying to stay open during the pandemic. One of the worst things about COVID-19 was how it isolated us all.

Our office emerged from the COVID-19 pandemic as a new office. We were better equipped to work remotely and learned to adjust protocols quickly. In addition, many tools, such as video meetings, became commonplace, and a blend of telework and office work was more common. I noticed some people didn't emerge from COVID-19 the same. Some wanted to continue staying home, some changed careers, and some didn't handle the stress well.

Reflecting on the changes experienced in the last five years alone leaves me utterly amazed. The uncertainty of what lay ahead lingered in my thoughts. In navigating the unknown, I prayed, seeking guidance, wisdom, and relief from stress as the sole means to navigate the challenges.

In my experience, the higher I climb in this field, the less time I spend on technical matters. This doesn't mean the technical work is less critical. It is more important in a management role. Leading the development of technical work and signing off and approving technical work is vital. A manager must also recall technical matters when interacting with executives and the public, whether at meetings, on camera, or otherwise. Other disciplines in a managerial role consist of change management, human resources, adaptive leadership, organizational development, policy, logistics, negotiation, and more. I needed to become proficient in all these categories to function well. Responding to COVID-19 required newly needed skill sets. I feel my background and disability helped me in the managerial role.

Chapter Twenty-Four

Did I Help Fish?

It should now be apparent that I believe God created me to be a fish biologist. In God's creation, everything is inherently good; the crucial factor lies in whether it is utilized to honor goodness or misused. Reflecting on over thirty years in my career, I can't help but ponder: 'Did I truly contribute to the well-being of fish?' Were the countless hours of paperwork and stress worthwhile? I answer this with an emphatic 'yes' for the following reasons.

Fish can't help themselves. They can't avoid destroyed habitats, get over dams, and successfully deal with high temperatures due to climate change without our help. Fish can swim out of harm's way—however, they aren't the smartest of animals, and if the problem is large-scale, such as temperature changes or ecosystem scale alterations, they can't avoid it. This is their home, and someone has to help them. Humans depend on the ecosystem for food, and fish are part of it. Commercial fisheries depend on salmon for their livelihood. In addition, recreational fishing is a tremendous industry and a significant economic driver. Future generations need a healthy ecosystem with fish. I chose to help.

Much of my career involved the study of fish. My development of agency reports, fisheries data, and peer-reviewed literature have been used by scientists worldwide. The information collected by our office(s) has been used by academia, government scientists, water operations managers, and industry consultants to better manage water operations and construction projects to protect fish. The information collected and stored has been used to establish Endangered Species Act listings for five fish species in the Central Valley of California. Said information will likely be used for additional listings in the future.

While at the National Marine Fisheries Service as a consultation biologist, I reduced the impacts of actions in our waterways that impacted listed species. Small victories were found in the negotiations with applicants, the requirement of mitigation measures, and the development of conservation measures. One project at a time, these beneficial things add up. I was one of two leads that listed green sturgeon under the Endangered Species Act, leading to changes in fishing regulations, the development of prohibitions, and other measures to benefit these fish for the future.

My testimony in front of state boards, county supervisors, and other venues informed many of the importance of fish and the ecosystem.

I was a cog in an extensive restoration wheel. I contributed to various projects by connecting with landowners, developing projects, helping with permits, evaluating documents, managing grants and deliverables, and critiquing restoration projects.

I was at the helm when the U.S. Fish and Wildlife Service spearheaded the release of delta smelt as a last-ditch effort to save the imperiled fish. Delta smelt were collected in the wild to produce a broodstock. They were reproduced in captivity, tagged, and released in the wild. All indications appear that the released delta smelt survived and even reproduced. I am convinced we saved the species from extinction.

My involvement in hiring, mentoring, and coaching the next generation of fish biologists helped build future fish biologists, furthering the protection of fish themselves. I hired veterans who served our country honorably and as diverse individuals, helping to create a new agency. The upcoming generation is brilliant, and I have complete confidence in their abilities. They will undoubtedly find solutions to challenges that eluded me. They must survive the bureaucracy and ensure it doesn't eat them up.

What an honor to have helped fish—animals that can't speak for themselves.

Chapter Twenty-Five

Parting Recommendations

Y ou have many demands on your time, and I am grateful you chose to read my memoir. I hope my journey offers lessons and insights for you, whether you are diagnosed with dyslexia, know a person with dyslexia, or are simply curious. I also believe my journey and coping mechanisms can be helpful for individuals with other disabilities. While I feel my journey with dyslexia is not over yet, it took me a long time to understand the impacts and benefits of this "disability" on my life. I can contextualize my difficult educational background, which is very satisfying. I provide some advice below.

As is often the case, when something is broken, we strive to fix it. Usually, only the specific broken part is repaired, leaving the more significant part broken and unchanged. For example, the alignment in your vehicle needs to be better calibrated, which causes your tires to wear quickly. You replace the tires, yet the vehicle alignment is still broken. The same can be said for dyslexia. A person can have the dyslexia diagnosis and attempt to fix or at least cope with the diagnosis. Often, this is a struggle over years and even decades, and great strides can be made with specialized treatment and assistance. Yet, the overall dyslexic condition is permanent, and one must adjust and cope with the lifelong condition. But what about the general human that has dyslexia? Is there a more significant problem?

Every person has one big problem that must be reconciled. Realizing one's full potential depends on reconciling one's purpose. Often, people try to fill this problem with success, money, purchasing fancy things, vacations, etc., but it can't be fixed with material things. The task is to find the creator to fill this hole. The creator is God.

The more significant problem is that humans are inherently sinful people. Humans are selfish, greedy, and dishonest. All of us are, including myself. God is not. God is perfect, and He sent His son, Jesus, to be sacrificed on the cross to pay the penalty for humanity's sins. This is God's way of offering forgiveness and eternal life to us. Jesus was crucified for our sins and, on the third day after, rose from the grave to be with God.

Accepting Jesus into your heart and understanding that God loves you and has a plan for your life is essential. Not only does this bring salvation and an eternity in heaven, but it also brings you hope as you will understand fully that you were made for a purpose. When we accept Jesus into our hearts, we become part of the kingdom of God. We are promised a life of eternity with God. I shared the power of prayer and the Holy Spirit in this book. I also talked about the Holy Bible and its vast knowledge base. Jesus will be your arsenal against the trials of life.

This book is about dyslexia and my battle with it. I believe God had a plan for me and blessed me with this condition. When I accepted Jesus into my heart, I took the command to spread His news. I firmly believe one cannot be a complete person without letting go and accepting that God is in control of one's life, and I genuinely believe that doing so will help your dyslexia journey or any life challenge. Your dyslexic condition will be thought of as an actual disability until you realize you were made for a purpose by God. Thus, my first and most crucial suggestion is to accept Jesus into your heart.

This suggestion is life-changing and the most important decision you will ever make, as this has to do with your soul. It is the acknowledgment that God created you for a purpose, fearfully and wonderfully, and that He loves you. In God's view, you are perfectly made. He should know because He made you! In the book of Matthew, Jesus describes how God knows and cares deeply about every human soul.

*[30]And even the very hairs of your head are all numbered. [31]
So don't be afraid; you are worth more than many sparrows.*
(Matthew 10:30-31, The Holy Bible, NIV)

There are no secret formulas or tricks to accepting Jesus. To do so, one needs to bow their head and say a prayer. For example, you could say, "Dear Jesus, please forgive me for my sins. I understand that You died for me so I could be with You for eternity. I want to turn my life over to You. I give my life to You, Jesus. Amen."

I would encourage you to connect with a group of believers at a local church. Perhaps you know someone who attends church? You can ask to go with them; they would love to have you! If attending in person is difficult, you can watch church services online.

Resilience is "an ability to recover from or adjust easily to misfortune or change."[1] People with dyslexia or other life challenges must develop resilience to weather the problematic circumstances over time. It takes considerable time and effort to navigate and overcome reading and writing difficulties. In addition, developing survival and coping skills takes time and effort. Research the stories of famous people who documented their backgrounds of dyslexia, and you will see the resilience need-

---

1. "Resilience." Merriam-Webster.com Dictionary, Merriam-Webster, https://www.merriam-webster.com/dictionary/resilience. Accessed 29 Dec. 2023.)

ed to navigate the challenges that span decades. You will have to navigate your dyslexia for some time before you bloom, and it will seem like you are surviving a misfortune; however, eventually, you will discover you also have special abilities.

Read about how people with dyslexia overcame the disability and found success, and one thing becomes clear: many of them had a series of helpers. Parents, teachers, coaches, and all helpers played a significant role in that person's discovery and journey. My parents worked with the school district to get me tested and sent to special day classes, and in addition, they sought private learning specialists to help me. If I hadn't received this help, there is no doubt I would have slipped through the cracks, and my future would not be the same. Advocates and supporters can also lift you up and assure you that you are not "stupid," helping you survive the problematic schooling. If you are suffering through dyslexia on your own—don't!

It is highly recommended that children's hobbies and interests be identified, as Sally Shaywitz described in her book *Overcoming Dyslexia*. According to her, it is critical to help children find an area of interest where they can have a positive experience, whether for pure enjoyment or the ability to excel. As Shaywitz says, this can be anything from "an interest in fish or rock collecting to talents such as baton twirling or juggling, skills in sports such as skating or swimming, talents like acting or drawing, an aptitude for understanding science or computers, or a love of poetry or music."

I shared my various hobbies and exploits in this book. I enjoy building things and discovering processes, which is a dyslexic tendency. My hobbies gave me an outlet to explore and display my dyslexic skills, and one of them led me to a career. I am forever grateful I was given the freedom to explore new things. Don't avoid the many benefits hobbies can bring a person with dyslexia.

Like hobbies, sports are a way to gain self-confidence and enjoyment outside the classroom. Dyslexia has little bearing on sports and evens the playing field. Teamwork, hard work, and practice all build character and can bene-fit one's life. Sports are an integral part of well-being and should be pursued.

If you understand the beast, you can tame the beast. It can be beneficial to learn about the dyslexic condition. Helping to understand the strengths and weaknesses in the school environment will provide countless benefits. Understanding the many strengths of dyslexia can help pinpoint college education and career choices. Learning about the condition can broaden your perspective and assist you with your journey. It will become clear that dyslexia has a negative and a positive side, and it isn't a bad thing. It can open up doors and opportunities. Learning about dyslexia can give you confidence and hope for the future.

I would like to hear about your journey. Most importantly, please share the good news with me if you accept Jesus. I would love to celebrate with you. The best way to reach me is via the contact form of my author website, Jeffrey mclain.com.

Acknowledgements

This book is about my struggle with dyslexia and how I persevered from a challenging academic past to a successful career in the sciences. This feat was not accomplished solely on my own but consisted of people from my family, coaches, teachers, mentors, friends, and more. I find it necessary to thank those who helped me through my life, as well as those who helped with this book.

My mom and dad, Georgi and George McLain (yes, this is true, these are their names), who have been married for more than 60 years, were fearless advocates for me as a child, and they continue to be to this day. They provided a remarkable, almost magical childhood where I could do what I wanted, whether converting my bedroom to an aquarium or building a fort in their backyard. It was my parents who provided an education and special care for my dyslexia and continuously filled my head with comments of affirmation, helping me cope with school difficulties. My mom and dad introduced me to Jesus by taking me to church as a child and then again to Europe, where I discovered God's call. Besides God, nobody has had more impact than my parents, and I am forever grateful.

Educators change lives, and this saying is especially true in my case. Without the dedication and support of numerous heroes along the way, I would likely have fallen through the cracks. I will thank the big ones here. I was a student of the Lafayette School District, and I attended Burton Valley Elementary School, Merriewood Elementary, Stanley Junior High School, and Campolindo High School. Each of these schools had my champions, and there are many. Sue Wiseman and Marta Hackney, two extraordinary women at Burton Valley, were my special day class heroes who helped me with my reading and comprehension. The school administrators welcomed me back to fourth grade at Merriewood Elementary and helped me assimilate.

Lola Danielle taught Spanish at Campolindo High School for 59 years, likely changing many lives. She was patient, understanding, and caring, which enabled me to survive two years of her class and develop study habits that would last a lifetime.

Dr. Joe Brumbaugh, my undergraduate advisor at Sonoma State University, spent valuable time reviewing test results with me and setting up special testing arrange- ments if needed. Anthony Tusler and Janis Parks of the Sonoma State University Disability Resource Cen- ter cared deeply for my education. They secured access to priority registration, testing aides, and other special arrangements and accommodations.

There are countless people that I have worked with over my career, and they taught me what to do and what not to do. My career development relates to the story of this book, and thus, I will thank those who had the most significant impact. My first boss in the professional world of fisheries biology was Dr. Marty Kjelson. Marty modeled Christian leadership in the workplace and set many examples. I am grateful for his support and guid- ance as I continue the Christian walk and, in addition, his example of leadership. Dr. Russ Bellmer was another former boss and mentor who encouraged me to step into leadership positions. I am thankful for his career advice and mentorship.

First Baptist Church of Lodi has shone God's light in the community and the world for over a century. I feel honored and blessed to be a part of such a church. My ears and heart have soaked up sermons and messages for over two decades, and I continue to witness the self- less service of countless others. Thank you, First Baptist Church, for spiritually feeding and grounding me. May God continue to bless you in the centuries ahead.

My friends walk through life with me. They are a shoulder to lean on and an ear to listen to. Glen Barnes, John Hunt, Eric Larson, Mark VanNess, and Mike Georguson, thank you for always being straight with me on Thursday mornings, telling me when I am going in the wrong direction, and guiding me in faith, work, and life.

Getting the ideas in my head to paper coherently was difficult, and several people helped. Furthermore, there are thousands of support choices in the author world, and I will give you several true professionals here. Amy Bee of Lion by the Tail Editing is a quick and insightful study. She provided much-needed early guidance on voice and formatting. I am thankful for Helen Baggott's developmental editing assistance and constant questions and suggestions about my gibberish. This undoubtedly made this book more readable and coherent. Thank you, Megan Tatreau of Purple Pencil, for making this book the best it could be and for your editorial expertise and professionalism.

I collaborated with Euan Monaghan, a Netherlands designer, and shared my book cover ideas with him. He created a stunning cover showing a contemplative boy surrounded by swimming fish. I am genuinely grateful for his exceptional creativity and expertise.

I thank my book launch team for their early review and insightful feedback. My friends and colleagues came through in a big way. Some of them routinely edit scientific work, and I suffered the wrath of their red pens, which improved my book. This was not the first time I was "garwinized" by Garwin Yip at NOAA's National Marine Fisheries Service!

I am grateful to have talented writers and editors in my family. Despite being only 18 years old, my youngest daughter, Sarah, found the time to offer some incredibly insightful edits. I also want to express my deep appreciation to Anne, my best friend and wife, for her unwavering patience and support. Thank you, Anne, for embracing my writing dream and for those late-night editing sessions.

Thank you, God, for creating me the way you did. Full of unique imperfections. Thank you for sending your son Jesus to walk the earth and being my redeemer!